In His Perfect Time
84 Devotions For Women Waiting on Marriage

Adalis Ayala

ISBN: 9781972421000(Paperback)

Any references to historical events, real people, or real places are used fictitiously. Names, characters, and places are products of the author's imagination.

Printed in the United States of America.

First printing edition 2026

Victorious Seeds Publishing

I'd like to dedicate this book to the following women of God that He has placed in my life to speak in to me, mentor me, help me grow and encourage me. I wouldn't be where I am if not For the Lord and you.

To Grandma Sara your unceasing faithful prayers have led me to Jesus, your presence and counsel encourage me and you know my heart. I know that you are always in my corner.

To Betty the mother of my heart, your silliness always reminds me to laugh and find joy and your unwavering confidence in me is divinely orchestrated, you see me an accept me whatever season, whatever mood.

To Althea, momma if not for you I don't believe I would have ever been able to step out of my comfort zones, believed in the anointing over my life or the capability of operating in my God given gifts. Thank you for always seeing me.

To Momma Patty, thank you for every prayer, every teaching, every prophetic impartation, every word you've spoken over me that breathed life and you didn't even know it, thank you for seeing me as your daughter.

Table of Contents

Marriage is a beautiful covenant between a man and a woman, with God at the center creating a threefold cord that cannot easily be broken.

Women of God, we are all in different stages in this marriage season. Some of us are just at the beginning stage in our marriage promise journey, and have just put in a prayer to Heaven. Praying to our Heavenly Father, letting Him know we desire marriage. Some of us have been called to marriage because our union will be a purpose filled ministry. Some of us are at the standing stage for a spouse that God has revealed to us, but is not quite ready to be brought to us because preparation; cleansing; healing, and submission are required first. Marriage is two separate individuals becoming one body in Christ. This can be challenging. It is important to know this truth going in.

This devotional is designed to take you on a journey of self discovery of who you are as an individual, and preparation of becoming one with a God ordained husband. The Bible verses chosen, the self examining questions placed in each devotional, the guided prayers are all strategically set up to help you discover any areas that require your healing, any areas where your focus has been on the desire for marriage but not the one who is the source of that desire in your heart-which is Father God.

As you make your way through each devotion and guided prayer you will come to understand that marriage is a selfless act of love, just as Jesus committed the most selfless act of love Himself. He died so we would live. Dying to self does not mean sacrificing ourselves, it means becoming whole alongside the man God has chosen for us. It is written that "it is not good for man to be alone", but it is also written that there was no mate to be found comparable to Adam-so God made Eve. God made her from Adam's own rib. The original owner of your rib is out there. My desire is that this devotional not only help you prepare for marriage, but that it helps you be patient in the waiting, that you take this waiting season as a time to

grow in your relationship with Jesus and form an unbreakable bond that sustains you- in challenging moments, and that even in marriage God is your source. He is the only one who can completely fulfill you. People will disappoint in moments, maybe not measure up, but God is the same yesterday, today and forever.

With Love,

Adalis

Father I just pray for my sister in Christ that as she commits to this season of waiting and preparation, and this journey of self discovery, that she recognizes that you Lord are her source, and that she can always depend on you. Lord help her to see the strengths she's bringing into this marriage covenant, to heal the wounded places and to pray that in areas that she is not as strong, that the husband-that you have chosen her for-can rise to the challenge and support and strengthen her in Jesus name. Amen.

Trusting God's Timing

Lovely sister in Christ, seasons can be hard in both the natural and the supernatural. In the natural there is the seasonal cycles of life and death. There are also the seasons of Spring, Summer, Fall, and Winter. In the spirit there are seasons that are appointed times. Appointed times to serve in certain ministries. Appointed times to be a leader. Appointed times to learn and to follow. Appointed times to wait. Appointed times for fulfillment of promises given by your heavenly Father. God has purposed a marriage for you, if that is the desire that He Himself has placed in your heart. If He has purposed it, then the appointed season for it will come. It may not be as fast as you would like it to be, you may grow weary at times in the waiting, but it is God's will to give you a "good thing" in "due season". Ecclesiastes says "a time to every purpose under Heaven". The word purpose there means pleasure. Marriage is a gift and a pleasure. It too will have its appointed times of growth, of challenges, of victories, the key is to trust Him. As you wait know that it is a preparation, not only for you but for the husband that God has chosen you for. Take the seasons as they come. Try not to waste your seasons complaining or begging God for it to be over, and instead allow yourself to be stretched and to grow. Think of the ocean waves, when the waves come in, they bring the blessings of God and when they flow away, they carry whatever imperfections you carry; whatever hurts; whatever shame; whatever darkness, the Lord had to wash away from you for you to be prepared. Seasons are a journey, learn and grow and take every opportunity the Lord lays at your feet.

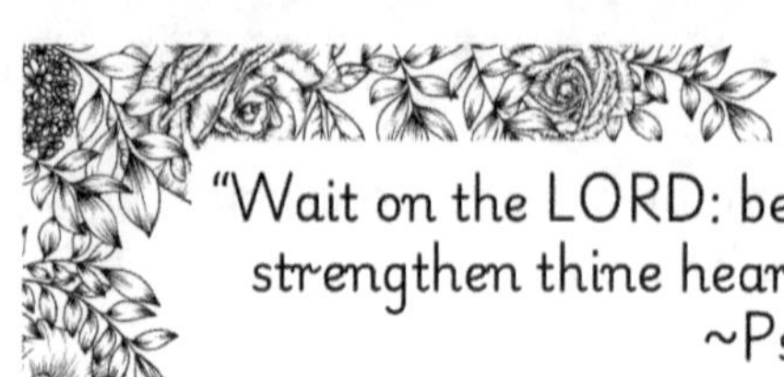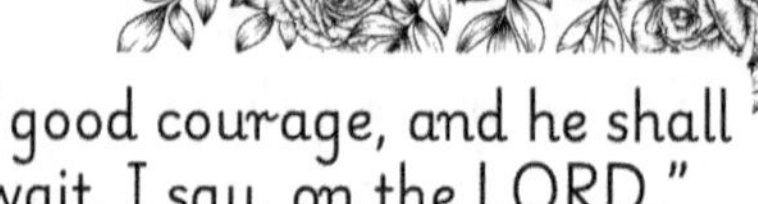

"Wait on the LORD: be of good courage, and he shall strengthen thine heart: wait, I say, on the LORD."
~Psalm 27:14

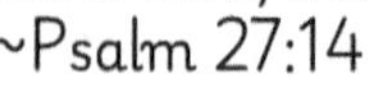

Waiting on the LORD, if we are honest with ourselves, can be hard. Waiting when our heart loses hope, can bring on despair. Being of good courage is difficult. Especially, when the LORD has only spoken the word of promise deeply within our hearts alone and we wait, and we wait for confirmation and it does not come. It does not come, not because you got it wrong. It does not come, not because He is withholding it from you. The confirmation does not come, because God is calling you to a deeper level of trust with Him. He wants you to lay down all walls and know in the deepest well of your being that He Himself has given you a promise. That He does not lie, because He cannot lie. That trusting Him will require a deeper level of courage, a level of deeper faith, than you've ever had before and if you just give Him a little more of your trust moment by moment He will strengthen your heart. As you wait, lay everything at His feet and never take things into your own hands. Wait on the LORD even when the moment feels too hard, or the moment feels like you can't take it anymore and wait another second. These are the perfect moments for breakthrough if we just surrender a little more, push a little harder despite how we feel. You will never regret a moment spent lingering and waiting on the LORD. He is a giver of good things. He is the Redeemer of His children.

"Trust in the LORD with all thine heart; and lean not unto thine own understanding. In all thy ways, acknowledge him, and he shall direct thy paths."
~Proverbs 3:5-6

Have you ever had trouble "leaning not unto thine own understanding?" I am physically raising my right hand up, and my inner child is jumping up and down saying "me, me, me." This is why the Word tells us to take "every thought captive." We need to reach a heart posture that turns away from our fleshly desire to want to know and understand the "why" of a situation. This has been the most difficult part of my journey. I trust the LORD with all my heart, I acknowledge Him in all my ways, and I know that I know that He directs my paths, but because there are moments where I do not take my thoughts captive-that I then find myself questioning the LORD. Do not be ashamed because we've all been there at some point. Repent and move on and be intentional about trusting God without boundaries separating you. When you lean on your own understanding you are creating a boundary that separates you from the LORD. If your understanding and your questioning is greater than your trust, then your heart posture is in the wrong place. The LORD wants you to trust Him, so that you learn to trust the head He is placing in your family. Trust that God's choice is the best choice. Trust that God's direction is the best direction. In this season of waiting and preparation learn to whole-heartedly trust God, and understand that "His ways are not our ways, and His thoughts are not our thoughts". He is so beyond what our minds can comprehend fully, and His eyes see beyond, and deeper than what our eyes ever could. Always acknowledge Him and never forget Him. He desires to be included in every way.

"But they that wait upon the LORD shall renew their strength; they shall mount up with wings as eagles; they shall run, and not be weary; and they shall walk, and not faint."
~Isaiah 40:31

LORD. Elohim you have created us in your image, and so because you have strength, we have strength. LORD, we know that because we wait upon you second by second, minute by minute and moment by moment that you are constantly and consistently renewing our strength. We faint not because you faint not. LORD, we will ascend with wings as eagles and allow your wind to sustain us in moments we cannot sustain ourselves. Especially when strong but weary of waiting. LORD, we shall run this race of preparation even when it feels like it is crawling at the pace of a snail, or even at a complete stand still- the gun not having gone off to signal the beginning of the race. Weariness will be but a distant memory when all that you have prepared us for comes to be and your word does not fail. LORD, we will walk until the finish line appears and we will continue to walk beyond it if you so call us to. EL Roi help us to never lose sight of you-because the season we are in becomes too much to bear and loneliness takes root, as you have never lost sight of us. In Jesus name we pray. Amen.

"For the vision is yet for an appointed time, but at the end
it shall speak, and not lie: though it tarry, wait for it;
because it will surely come, it will not tarry."
~Habakkuk 2:3

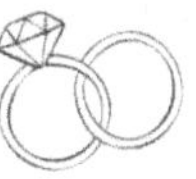

Timing is important. Not our timing but God's timing. Sis,
you know that God's timing is always perfect. How much
easier would the wait be, if we focused on the vision that
accompanies the word the Lord has spoken to us, rather
than counting the minutes that have passed without the
fulfillment. Counting the minutes just drags on the passage
of time. Psalms 90:4 says, "A thousand years in your
sight are like a day that has just gone by". What does that
tell us? That God is time itself, but He is not subject to it.
What do you think matters most to God? The period
you've waited? Or the completion of the preparation He
has ordained for you? The end of the waiting will all lead
to one thing. That what God has said, is what will be, and
it will be proven to be everything He said it would be. If we
ourselves appointed the time, can you just imagine the hot
mess it would be? It would be a mad dash to the altar, we'd
probably still be wearing slippers, our bath robe, rollers in
our hair with one lash on and one lash off. What a comedy
of errors, but with God. My God, My God, it would be
class and sophistication, love and peace, beyond all that we
could possibly imagine. Let him prepare you into the
beautiful bride, wife and helpmate He destined for you to
be. In the long run it will be for your benefit and the
benefit of your husband. God doesn't do the little picture
He does the whole art gallery. When It tarries in
purposeful productivity, then it does not tarry at all.

"For my thoughts are not your thoughts, neither are your ways my ways, saith the LORD. For as the heavens are higher than the earth, so are my ways higher than your ways, and my thoughts than your thoughts."
~Isaiah 55:8-9

LORD thank you that your thoughts are not my thoughts. If I were to be honest with myself, I'd admit that my thoughts at times can be selfish and self-centered. There are times when my thoughts are angry and self-serving. There are times when my thoughts are insecure and unworthy. I am thankful LORD, that because your thoughts are higher and more powerful, that when I cry out to you the lies of the enemy cannot take root, and again my thoughts are taken captive and my sight is set on you. Thank you LORD that your thoughts know and show the way that this marriage will come together in your time, and that because I trust in you, although my thoughts are not the same- that the outcome shall be fruitful. LORD thank you that my ways are not your ways, because it teaches me to rely on your way as the ONLY way. Thank you that my ways are not your ways because I, in my not so infinite wisdom would make a mess out of things. Thank you, Almighty God, that your ways and your thoughts are higher than mine, because your eagle vision can perceive and process things that my limited human mind could not contain. I am thankful that you LORD are you and I am simply me. My less becomes more when in your capable hands. Thank you because you see why you have called this specific husband as my partner. Thank you because you have selected this marriage in your infinite wisdom, to bring glory to your name and kingdom in ways that I have not even conceived of yet. Thank you for revealing my thoughts

and ways to the husband you have chosen for me in the best light so that he understands what a blessing I will be as his helpmate. Thank you that you reveal the thoughts and ways of my God ordained husband to me so that I may better understand how to submit to, pray for, respect, honor, and help him as you have called me to do. LORD your desire is for us to soar to new heights with you, so we must depend upon your ways and your thoughts revealed moment by moment at appointed times. In Jesus name we pray. Amen.

"Be still, and know that I am God: I will be exalted among the heathen, I will be exalted in the earth."
~Psalm 46:10

When you are behind the wheel of a car you are in control of the destination, you are in control of the speed at which you travel and the stops you make along the way. Because you are in control there is no reason to fear, no reason to be anxious except maybe for traffic. You are at peace because you are in control. Walking in the Spirit requires us to let go of control and hand it over to God instead. To "Be still and Know that He is God" means to quiet yourself, in mind, body and spirit. It means to stop working so hard to attain what you are chasing after, and acknowledge that God is the one in control. You may be sitting in the car behind the wheel, but He is the one steering. It can be nerve wracking, but if you know that God will never lead you into danger, never lead you into the dark, never lead you to a place or person that you will find yourself lost and without signal, then anxiety will never take root in your mind, body or spirit. Bringing yourself to stillness and acknowledging that He is God brings you peace in challenging moments; through trials and tribulations; through weariness. You are letting go of your human limitations and trading it for the full recognition of His power and His presence in every aspect of your life. Let me tell you, nothing you can say to the husband God has chosen for you-if you are in communication- will bring him closer to you, will change his heart toward you, while you wait. Only surrendering control to God will be the propulsion so that things come into play and move in the correct direction. When we finally come together with the men of God, He has chosen us for, the Lord will be exalted. Look within yourself and ask Holy Spirit if you are being still and knowing that He is God. If you are not, ask Him how to surrender your will and your control. He is faithful to do just that. Holy Spirit is our teacher, and He is also our comfort.

Do you know that God not only sees you, but He hears you
as well. I know that there have been times in my walk with
Him that I have truly, in an unguarded moment, felt that
my prayers were falling on deaf ears. We can only move
forward and grow if we are willing to be honest with
ourselves and with God. At the end of the day there is not
one thing or thought that God does not know about you. My
mother likes to tell me that she pictures the angles in heaven
writing quickly as they write down every never-ending
stream of conversation and thought that I throw out at God.
Some of the things I say shock her. I always say I imagine
said angels shaking their heads and saying, "there she goes
again God. Talking about that marriage promise. Is it time
to send him yet?" I laugh out loud mostly to myself when the
imagery hits me. Our answers to everything in life are there
if we just look up to the LORD. Our God hears us, but are
we listening when He responds, or are we dismissing His
voice because it is not the answer we want at that given
moment? I've been there. When God gives you a word and
it's not the one you think you need or the one you want at
that moment. We forget that God knows what we need right
when we need it. A word of hope when that last shred of hope
we have is dying. His gentle presence in the middle of a
storm of a situation. Peace when we ourselves are out of
control. Maybe right now God is not telling you much about
the husband He has for you but if you just get in His will, He
may give you direction in how to pray for him. Maybe right
now you don't know specifically the man God has chosen,
but you know that He has given you a marriage promise.
Instead of asking who, ask the right question. "Lord how do

you want me to pray for this man?" And when you are praying for that husband ask God to change you as He changes him more and more into His image. But most of all Remember to Thank God for choosing the very best for you, His daughter, and for salvation for not only you but the husband as well.

"The LORD is good unto them that wait for him, to the soul that seeketh him. It is good that a man should both hope and quietly wait for the salvation of the LORD."
~Lamentations 3:25-26

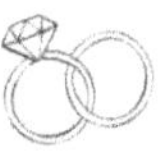

Above our desire for the marriage promise should be our desire for God. A marriage promise can become an idol if we are not careful. Our eyes should always be on the promise giver not the promise itself. It says in this verse that "it is good that a man should hope...". Hope is a gift given to us from Jesus Himself. It is also written in Psalm 33:22, Colossians 1:27, Psalm 62 and Matthew 12:21 that our hope is always in Jesus Himself. If He is our high priest who always makes intercession for us as it is written in Hebrews 7:24-25, then when our hope is in Him then every good thing that our heavenly Father has willed for us will come to His desired and preordained conclusion. Lamentations tells us to "quietly wait for the salvation of the LORD". We need to be sure that we are not expecting this husband to fill the Role of God in our life and be our salvation. The husband is not our salvation. The husband is a good gift, but he cannot save you or redeem you. He will be a good gift and a good shepherd leading you back to Christ, but not your savior. We must be very careful, and not lose sight of who our true salvation lies in. Keep your eyes and your heart on God, let Jesus intercede for you to the heavenly Father. As you quietly wait for the salvation of the LORD, also quietly sit in the presence of God and let your heart speak its hope. God hears the cry of your heart. Always.

You may ask yourself from time to time how can I rejoice in hope, when my eyes have yet to see what I am hoping for. What I say in response is, "Faith is the substance of things hoped for and the evidence of things not yet seen". You cannot lose your faith. Be intentional about rejoicing and celebrating, even if your eyes have not seen it yet, your spirit knows it is on the way. The tribulation that comes as you wait has one name and one name only. "DOUBT". It is the biggest attack of the enemy in waiting seasons. "DOUBT" that you discerned the word from God correctly. "DOUBT" that you are worthy to receive a marriage promise when you believe you are still a mess and undeserving. This last point has been me on and off again during this process. I grew up in a household where I had to walk on eggshells and try to fly under the radar and not garner attention, because the attention of one of my parents was not the good kind. I grew up feeling that no matter what I did I still was unworthy. It was a long process for me to overcome this childhood curse. During this tribulation period called DOUBT be intentional about dismissing it from your vocabulary and your thoughts. Have patience with yourself because it will not come overnight. And last but never least, don't stop praying. The minute you stop praying tribulation will take hold and next thing you know the rejoicing well and celebration inside of you will have dried up. Stay connected to your source.

Finding Contentment In Singleness

"Not that I speak in respect of want: for I have learned, in whatsoever state I am , therewith to be content."
~Philippians 4:11

Lord we as your daughters, come before you with the petitions in our hearts for the godly men you have chosen and prepared us for, let us be content with the waiting. Let us be content with where you have positioned us on this journey. Let us be in peace of mind, heart, and spirit knowing that our daddy in Heaven has us just where we need to be, as well as our husbands, and when we need to be there. The concern we have in our hearts over the delays, the stumbling blocks, the weariness, also concerns you and because it concerns you, we know and acknowledge that everything is in your hands and though we may not see it, you are still working behind the scenes. You are not an absent Father. You are ever present. Contentment is an intentional action, not just a feeling. Help us Lord to be intentional about being positive, and not focusing on the negative parts of the journey. We will choose today to be content. In Jesus mighty name we pray. Amen.

"You will show me the path of life;
In Your presence is fullness of joy;
At Your right hand are pleasures forevermore."
~Psalm 16:11

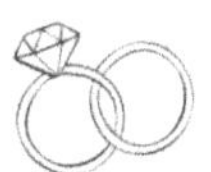

All of our direction comes from God. There are times when we need to take a step of faith or a step of obedience and then He will "show" us where we need to head next. Remember Abraham? What did the LORD say to him? "Now the Lord had said to Abram: "Get out of your country, from your family and from your father's house to a land that I will show you." When Abraham set out, he had no clue where he was headed, but he stepped out in faith and obedience. Waiting doesn't mean just sitting and expecting God to do all the work while you sit and wait for a knock on the door or the ringing of the doorbell. There is such a thing as "active" waiting. Even in the waiting God will ask you to step out in faith and obedience. "Active" waiting doesn't mean waiting until your husband comes along to begin walking in your purpose, it means to begin walking in it while you wait. When you have moments that your hope fails, moments that you feel weary, moments that you begin to doubt your discernment, get into the presence of God and let Him restore your joy to overflowing. We must Keep our eyes on Him. No single person or thing will bring us Joy like Jesus. Nothing will complete us or fill us like He can. If we put our dependency on someone to make us happy or joyful, we will become disillusioned because we are putting our dependency on something that is flawed, or incapable of perfection. The only unfailing one is Jesus. The only perfect one is Jesus. We must strive to keep our position at the right hand of Jesus. Just like He maintains His place at the right hand of our Heavenly Father. Stay in His presence and in His sphere of influence, blessing and direction.

"But I would have you without carefulness. He that is unmarried careth for the things that belong to the Lord, how he may please the Lord: But he that is married careth for the things that are of the world, how he may please his wife. There is difference also between a wife and a virgin. The unmarried woman careth for the things of the Lord, that she may be holy both in body and in spirit: but she that is married careth for the things of the world, how she may please her husband. And this I speak for your own profit; not that I may cast a snare upon you, but for that which is comely, and that ye may attend upon the Lord without distraction."
~ 1Corinthians 7:32-35

Priorities. Our number one priority should be and always be God, and His kingdom. Have you ever noticed what happens when we start to get distracted and start to let other things in life take the number one spot in our priorities, and God gets shifted to the back burner? The first thing I notice in this situation is that my mood gets dark, negative emotions start to take the place of my joy and my sense of being fulfilled in Christ, and then other things start to turn upside down. My kids behaviors, my interactions with people, my sleep etc. What happens to cause you to notice that you've taken your relationship with God for granted and you've pushed Him to the back burner? It is easy to rectify. Repent and go back to making Him number one. In marriage, if you begin to put your spouse and family above God you will notice it because it will start to have challenges come up that will affect your marital relationship. It opens a door for satan to come in and wreak havoc. You must remember your relationship with God is your individual relationship, your relationship with your spouse is apart from that, but you will still need to put God in the center as the head over both. Don't ever trade God for your husband. It could become a catastrophe. God should always be first.

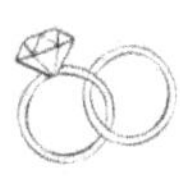

Are you seeking the kingdom of God first in your walk with God? It is a daily requirement to grow and maintain your relationship with God. It is a necessary must do in order for you to walk holy and righteous. If you don't seek the kingdom of God and His righteousness, how can you expect for His blessings, His direction, His anointing to flow in your life? You cannot expect God to send a godly, anointed, submitted, blessed man of God into your life for you to marry, if you yourself are not any of those things. I'm not saying you must be completely perfect in all those areas, but you do need to be in the process of working to shift in those areas of your life. For example, you may not be an intercessor but you do have the beginnings of a steady prayer life. That is an example of being in the process. It is written that "God's grace is sufficient." Have grace for yourself when you are not as strong in some of these areas as you are at other times, because you are still in the process of growing. God honors growth. God sees that you are trying. I am that kind of woman, that as soon as I wake up, there's either a worship song on my lips and I'm singing to God first thing, or I begin to speak to Him and thank Him for His goodness. I don't always get to my bible first thing but I do search Him out. You may seek Him in a different way and that is perfectly alright. If we were all cookie cutter replicas in how we sought God life would be just a boring routine. When we seek Him first, we shall see His goodness

show up all over our lives. I can't testify all the ways His goodness has followed me all my days up to today and how many more blessings are on the way. It would take several books. What things do you want God to add to you as you wait and seek His kingdom first? Not the husband but what other thing would you like Him to add to you? I can think of one very big thing even as I sit here writing this devotional. I know that it will come in His timing. God has never failed me because He is incapable of failure. Our relationship with God is reciprocal. If we give Him our FIRST of everything, if we seek Him and His kingdom FIRST, these things shall be added unto us. Do it with your whole heart, and not because you just want God to reciprocate. Remember He knows your heart and He cannot be fooled.

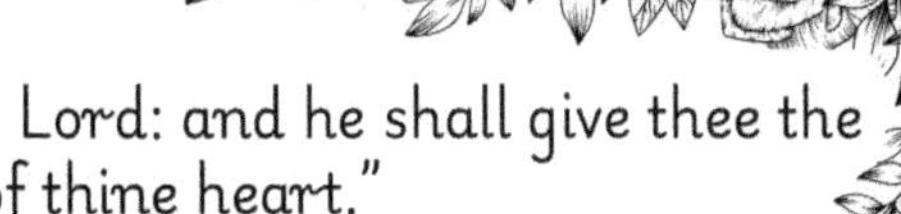

"Delight thyself also in the Lord: and he shall give thee the desires of thine heart."
~Psalm 37:4

In this scripture the word "Delight" is the Hebrew word, anag. In the Strong's Concordance it is #6026, which means "to be soft or pliable." What comes to mind as I reflect on this, is the Lord as the master potter. Have you ever seen a lump of clay, molded into beautiful pieces? That lump of clay is shaped and made pliable by adding water and shaping it with hands on the wheel as it spins. If we make it a point to enter the presence of God and make ourselves open and vulnerable. If we make ourselves soft and pliable then we can allow His presence to shift mold and change us, and that process becomes a delight, because our willingness is the core of that moment. We must remember that most of the desires of our heart come from the Father Himself. He desires to give us good things so then our heart desires to have those good and wonderful things. Let us not only be willing to allow God to shape our hearts and lives but let us be willing to allow Him to shape our desires more in alignment with His desire for us. The waiting allows us to spend time in His presence so that He may shape us more into the partner and helpmate that our husbands will require, but we must take delight in the process. If we don't learn to take joy in the process then our heart posture will never be in the correct position, causing delays or an unfulfilled promise and it won't be on God. It will be on us. "Delight Yourself in the LORD."

People pleasing is a real thing. I honestly believe it is something that takes hold of us when we are children. We want our parents to be proud of us. We want our friends to think that we are cool. We want our siblings to see us as the leader of the group. People pleasing is a hard bondage to break free from. If we are not careful, it follows us into adulthood. As an adult people pleasing can be made worse by our need for reassurance from the people closest to us. Reassurance that we are a good parent. Reassurance that we are doing a great Job. Reassurance that we are anointed and gifted. When we put the desire of reassurance over what God says, then we are in a dangerous position. I grew up walking on eggshells always trying to please a mom that could not be pleased. I grew up telling God I didn't want to be anything like her when I grew up. It took me a long time to break free of that need to be reassured. I still have moments, but it no longer controls the narrative of my life. One sure way to do things "heartily, as to the Lord," would be inviting the Holy Spirit into your day; into your schedule; into your life and asking Him to help you do things the way God would desire you to do things. He is your greatest help. When you are finally married if you live your life constantly wanting to please and reassure your spouse you will create a toxic environment. Hear me carefully. I'm not saying not to respect them or do kind things for them or give them compliments. Always examine your motivation. You want these acts to come from a pure heart not with the motivation to please, because if you don't, then there will be negative repercussions. This would cause you to live in anxiety, fear and stress that could then strain your marriage. If you are a people pleaser, open your heart to God and let Him heal that painful need so that you can love freely and without conditions.

Who is the giver of our peace? It's Jesus. If He is our peace
then it would be reasonable to say that it would be perfect.
In John 14:27 it is written "Peace I leave with you; my peace
I give to you; not as the world gives do I give to you. Let not
your heart be troubled, neither let it be afraid." This
teaches us that if we focus our attention higher during
times of struggle; of challenges and tribulations-to Jesus
the giver of peace-that perfect peace will come because we
trust in Him. Waiting can be the least peaceful thing
sometimes, but only because in our minds we try to see if
we can identify how God is trying to move the pieces in our
situation around. I know I'm guilty of this. We try in our
flesh to turn things in our favor by getting ahead of God or
interfering trying to make His promises happen on our
timing and not His timing. None of these things will give us
perfect peace because our heart posture is focused on the
"thing" or "person" rather than the giver. Elohim knows
every little part of you, because He created you there's a
deep connection at your core to Him. Because of this
connection, He knows what to say to you, how to touch
your heart in a specific way that will immediately bring you
perfect peace. Have you ever been in tears and suddenly,
the shalom of God came over you and your tears dried in
an instant? I'm so thankful for those moments when His
perfect Peace comes into the room and settles my thoughts.
If we can just learn to give up our need to control and learn
to turn everything over to Him instead, His perfect peace
would reign over our life.

"But godliness with contentment is great
gain"
~1Timothy 6:6

Waiting seasons are open doors for us to grow more devoted to God daily. Godliness is more than a state of mind; it is about living a life of honor and devotion to God. Devotion to God is shown in the fruit, from our commitment to walk in holiness. Waiting can also be seen as a test of our contentment. Are we truly satisfied with what we have or in what God has already given us? Are we desiring more because of our outward circumstances or because of the assurance inside each one of us, of God's divine providence. When I first started this marriage Journey it was for selfish reasons. God gave me the word that He was giving me a husband, but just beginning a divorce process at the time I was not emotionally or mentally prepared for God's promise. I was not a person who was content. I was drier than any desert. I was worn out, angry, and all I could think about was that I didn't ever want to get married again. I actually said "no God" the minute He gave me the word. I didn't want to trust any man with my life, my needs my emotions or the well-being of my children again. Then, as I began to walk this out with God; it was an I need a husband because I'm struggling as a single mom and don't want to do this parenting thing alone anymore type of thought process. It was the —let's be honest here- don't want to live without sex for the rest of my life here type mental thought process. It was the I want to stop suffering financially type of mental thought process. That obviously meant my heart posture was in the wrong place. I was only seeing the carnal needs I wanted met. When you reach the point-of laying it all down at the feet of Jesus- and letting Him then intercede for you to your Father in heaven, then you begin to change, and the more you lay it down the more that contentment replaces all the hurt the pain and the carnal needs. Godliness then steps in and transforms your thoughts, in alignment with the thoughts of God and Holy Spirit then leads you in all godliness and divine contentment and your desires from your soon to happen marital relationship change. It becomes about what you will sacrifice so that this incoming marriage will bring glory to the kingdom of God. It'll turn from the fear of what you will lose into the contentment that will be gained if you walk it out with a godliness mindset. Your needs will still be met. I learned in this period of waiting, that my husband will be a friend and confidant for our son, but he will also show him the struggles and the power to overcome as a man of God. I learned that he would show our daughter what to expect from a godly husband and not to settle for less than God's best. I say ours because my children from my previous marriage will become ours. Single mommas' let this godly husband share the burden, responsibility and upbringing for your children. Trust God and him. Let fear and expectation go and let godliness and contentment step in and fill the void left behind.

"Casting all your care upon Him, for He cares for you."
~1 Peter 5:7

Father in heaven, I come to you with the weight of the world on my shoulders. I come to you in my frustration and in my doubt. I come to you with my hurt, my shame, my agony and my fear. I cast it all at the feet of Jesus. I take the hand of your most precious son and come to you in the throne room of grace, and the mercy seat of heaven. Jesus and I place my cares upon you because you care for me, and for my situation. There is nothing that has escaped your eye, because you know the number of hairs on my head. I seek you fervently every minute and every hour knowing that you have the answer. Your son, and my savior, Jesus is the answer and there is nothing about me or any of my petitions that He has not already come to you with beforehand. Now we come together, hand in hand and say "Father step in, because I no longer want to handle things on my own. Father, I want to trust you. Father I'm clinging to the hem of Jesus garment and to His nail scarred hand knowing that He died for me but also gave me access to you. Thank you because I need not feel ashamed to come to you because you would never condemn me for sharing all that is in my thoughts and in my heart. Thank you because you care far more than just enough, and that you always hear my cry. Thank you for caring about me so much; about bringing me back into your embrace that you sent your ONLY begotten son to die for me. The Love you have for me as your daughter is unlike any I have previously known or any that is yet to come into my life but I know that I know, that the man you have chosen will be a reflection of your love for me, and as long as I keep that as a forefront in my mind all will be well.

God's Promises
&
Faithfulness

"For I know the thoughts that I think toward you, says the Lord, thoughts of peace and not of evil, to give you a future and a hope."
~Jeremiah 29:11

Isn't it wonderful that we have the thoughts that God thinks towards us written down like a love story. That when doubts arise-as a result of the enemy of our soul attacking us- we can go directly to His written word, the bible, and be reassured of our standing. Imagine if we were at war with God and the chaos that it would bring to our life. If that were the case, then all the thoughts He would have would be to destroy us because He regretted creating us in the first place. That has happened before. Remember Noah. God in that time regretted making mankind. I don't want Elohim ever to regret creating me. I'm so thankful that His grace and the blood of Jesus covers me. That when He thinks of me it's all about the good things He has in store. Not only that, but also His good thoughts about me because many times our thoughts and opinions of ourselves fall short. Not just the blessings but the hope for better days and better things. It's the hope that does it for me. Hope is my love language-if such a love language exists. If I have an unrelenting hope that I know without a shadow of a doubt that His thoughts and plans for me are to help me grow, and flourish under His care; grace; and love, so that I can be given a bright future than I have peace. If you ever have a moment when you are married and you are going through a rough patch, instead of looking for your feelings to be validated by a someone go back to God's written instruction, His love story written just for you and it will bring you back to a place where you understand He is the ultimate source of all things. His plans are to give you peace and not evil a hope and a future even if in that moment it does not feel like it. It is a promise you can count on again and again. What God thinks trumps everything else. Not saying that your spouse's opinion or thoughts don't matter, but bring them before God and allow Him to help you discern them and direct you in what you should do. Never let them become a weapon or the first brick of a wall of separation. Let God bring you back to the peace that surpasses all understanding.

> "And we know that all things work together for good to those who love God, to those who are the called according to His purpose."
> ~Romans 8:28

First things first. Know that you are "called according to His purpose". We as children of God love those God moments when everything falls into place, because we know down to our marrow that if we love Him, He is going to work it all out. That is a good thing to be sure of, but will you drown if there comes a time in your marriage walk when the "work together for good to those who love God" doesn't happen instantaneously? We need to remain grounded in our interpretation of this verse. I'll give a little testimony here to give you understanding. About 12 years ago God gave me a prophetic promise that I would conceive a son within a year. It happened how God said. At about seven months, I encountered some issues with my blood pressure. At my appointment I was told to drive directly to the hospital because they had found protein in my urine and my blood pressure was high. I did what they said, but with kind of a braggy attitude. My thought was "oh well God promised baby Jeremiah to me so the issue will be resolved quickly, and I'll go home." My other thought was "well the word says that all things work together for those who love the Lord." I got to the hospital and the situation was more urgent than I thought. My blood pressure was at stroke levels, which I wasn't told at my appointment. I was admitted. They said if the IV drugs fixed my blood pressure and protein issue then I could go home. After some hours everything was resolving itself only to take a turn for the worse. I had an option. Do the cesarean at that hospital and send the baby by ambulance to a hospital an hour away and we would be separated, or both of us go to a hospital with a Nicu. Of course, I chose the second option. What followed over the next twenty-five days was really a show of God's mercy and grace, but it was also a very humbling experience for me. Baby Jeremiah was born a preemie at three pounds ten ounces, and spent eighteen days in the hospital, when the doctors said it would be a six month stay. That is a story for another day. But God. Won't He do it! Jeremiah will be twelve this year. At the time I clung to my love for God, His grace and mercy, and although things didn't work out right away they did eventually. I'll ask you this. Are you walking in His purpose for your life? Don't search for purpose after you're married. It will cause you to flounder if you put the expectation on your life partner to help you FIND your purpose. That is God's job. Find God's purpose for your life before you enter your marriage so that you never have to seek validation and don't find yourself struggling to meet the expectations you set for yourself.

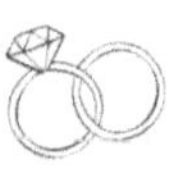

Isn't it amazing to know that God's mercies never fail and that His steadfast love is something that we can always depend upon? Neither His mercies nor His steadfast love ever come to a point where it ceases. God is always trying to draw us back to Him, even in our darkest hours where we in our rawness and our pain-at times-blame Him even when He is blameless. God is an enduring and unchanging God. Hebrews 13:8 tells us that "God is the same yesterday, today and forever" with great emphasis. Think about the mercies of your Father in heaven. His compassion for ALL is unfailing; boundless; without restraint. Being that His mercies are new every morning means we can rely on them being renewed each and every day, giving us hope and a fresh start. Sometimes I wake up feeling like I need a redo of the previous day, either because it did not go as planned or because I made poor decisions that I regretted. Aren't we so thankful that He does not hold on to our mistakes from yesterday as long as we repent. God's character is unlike the character of mankind. When we feel hopeless, we can count on Him to restore our hope. That is His faithfulness. When we lack the ability to trust others we can rely on the trustworthiness of His character. That is His faithfulness. When we need someone but can't find anyone, we can rely on the reliability and dependability of His character. That is His faithfulness. Now knowing these things about God think on how you can emulate the mercies of God in your future marriage? We can live life deciding not to go to bed angry, live a lifestyle of forgiveness and choose to love in a boundless way, even when things aren't perfect, so that we are not consumed by the agenda of the enemy. We can be intentional and choose to have compassion for others including our future husbands, and not just stop there but extend it to others. Being intentional will eventually reach the point where it just becomes a part of who you are. Isn't it just a blessing to know that each morning is an opportunity to start again. Maybe yesterday we could have said something to hurt or break our husband's spirit but today is a new day to make up for it by putting our best foot forward, apologizing and doing better. Maybe yesterday you don't show them allot of love or affection but today is an opportunity to give them a double portion. Maybe your husband really wanted to talk to you about something on their heart, but you didn't take the time to hear them out, but today you can make it a point to listen before you do anything else. Take the time to emulate the mercies, compassion, hope, trustworthiness and unfailing love of God's character to help your incoming marriage grow.

"God is not a man, that He should lie, Nor a son of man, that He should repent. Has He said, and will He not do? Or has He spoken, and will He not make it good?"
~Numbers 23:19

God I'm sorry. Sorry if I have become weary and doubtful of all that you have spoken to me. Sometimes it's just so hard Lord. I know that I give this marriage promise to you and then I take it back, help me to have serenity for what I cannot control. Help me to live out my faith according to your will and your timing. I don't want the promise before it is ready for me, help the impatience of my flesh to want it with a microwave quickness. Prepare me O Lord the way you prepared Esther. Help me become a woman of compassion, dedication, steadfastness. A woman that even when I fear, I push through anyway, always in obedience and with the willingness to do your will before all things. Help me be a symbol of hope, for my family and the man you have chosen to become my husband. Lord, I have seen you do all that you have promised before. I know that in this season of waiting and preparation, when you have deemed me ready; have deemed my earthly king ready- that you will again. I can trust and believe in your track record, but even yet I seem to go back and forth in my mind. Never in my heart. I know that double mindedness is not of you, release me from this stronghold on my mind Lord. O God help any unbelief I have and speak louder than the voice of the enemy that is trying to get me to give up my stand for my marriage promise. Bring me to a place in my spirit my Father in heaven where I know that I know without a shadow of a doubt that what you have said you will do, no matter my thoughts or how my flesh may feel. I know that because you have said it, I can believe it. Lord let that be the meditation of my heart and my mind. In Jesus mighty name Amen.

"Therefore know that the Lord your God, He is God, the faithful God who keeps covenant and mercy for a thousand generations with those who love Him and keep His commandments; "
~Deuteronomy 7:9

God is a covenant keeping God, so you can be assured that every promise as long as it comes directly from Him will be answered. It will never be broken. He will also have mercy on you as you wait so that you do not despair. Do you know that although your flesh may despair that your spirit will not, as long as you are connected to God, and aligned to His will. Even if the promise the Lord makes you is one that you will not get to see with your own eyes because it is a covenant that involves the generations that come after you, they will eventually come to pass. Remember that everything has its appointed time. Abraham did not get to see ALL of the promises he was given by God come to pass in their entirety, but he did get to witness the seed from which the covenant blessing would come from. Ask yourself, at this point in the waiting timeline, where in the meter does your love for God sit? Has the promise overtaken the place of your God? Has it taken the need for you to walk in obedience to His commandments away? Know that if you have put marriage or the husband He has chosen for you over Him, into an idolatrous position, then He will bring you into a place where He will prune that off of you. He is a jealous God. You can't just know OF God to have a covenant relationship; you have to take the initial steps to actually get to know Him. Your

relationship with Him will be the blueprint to your relationship with your husband. If you don't build your relationship with God Himself, how will you build a relationship with a husband or in a marriage? A marriage is a covenant relationship that will not just affect the two of you but also everyone tied to you. I encourage you, in this time of waiting to go before your Father in Heaven and seek His face asking Him if there is anything in your relationship with Jesus that needs to be rectified, so that when you enter covenant marriage there are no major stumbling blocks and you know to follow the blueprint of your heavenly relationship. Love Him and keep His commandments written on your heart. Those commandments are your blueprint for life. Never disregard them, they still exist, and He has never abolished them.

"The Lord is not slack concerning His promise, as some count slackness, but is long suffering toward us, not willing that any should perish but that all should come to repentance."
~2 Peter 3:9

Long suffering is something only daughters of God but also the people of God could learn. When we think of long suffering in our flesh what comes to mind is a long-drawn-out trial, test or tribulation but in reality, that is not it at all. In actuality, it is what God Himself modeled to us through scripture. Patience, which I will admit I lack more often than not. Do you? Slow to anger. I can admit God is still working on me in this area too. I have a long fuse but often a bad blow up, but the truth is that allot of us depending on the situation can be the same. Being long suffering towards us means that God Himself undergoes our failings with all of His grace but yet He gives us the time and the chance to come back to ourselves and repent making things right again. This chance gives us the time to grow, and it also shows us that we undergo punishment for our sins not because He desires to punish us but because there are consequences to that sin. Now think about your relationships in the past for just a moment and use it as a catalyst for change where needed. In past relationships did you walk in all that is long suffering? Patience, a slowness to anger; enduring the failings of your partner and yourself; showing grace and repentance; giving time for growth as a partnership; in repentance for actions taken; did you take time to think before lashing out in retaliation? It is allot to examine but it is very much needed, because you do not want to enter a life time commitment when you are still unhealed from past mistakes or the lack of long suffering because your personality type is the kind where you run when things get hard and you just quit. I completely understand trust me.

I've been there before. Sometimes even Longsuffering won't do it, and that's when you need to allow God to step in with direction. The old me was long suffering to the point I stopped and turned a blind eye to what I needed in the relationships until that long fuse exploded in very bad ways. I had to let God work on me and Heal me. Today communication and Relying on God is what keeps me from returning to old roles.

"Not a word failed of any good thing which the Lord had spoken to the house of Israel. All came to pass."
~Joshua 21:45

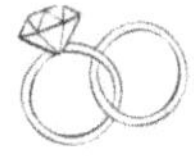

Lord, all throughout the scripture we see time and again that every word that proceeded out of your mouth never failed. Not if it was a good thing and neither if it was required judgement. Your word never falls to the ground or returns to you void. Lord thank you because every good thing that you have spoken to me and over me will not fail. Thank you because it will all come to pass. Lord my heart has so many answered prayers and promises to be thankful for. If there is ever a time that I have forgotten to thank you I am thanking you now. Lord thank you for being so faithful that you take the time to honor everything that you speak. All honor and glory belongs to you King Jesus. I am so thankful that your priestly intercession over my life and my person never ceases, even after your promises are fulfilled you never stop. You are always working even when I don't see it or can't see it. In my moments where my flesh becomes weak, and my thoughts become unaligned with yours let the memories of all the answered and fulfilled prayers and promises run like a video memorial in my thoughts with the reminder that if you did it before you will surely do it again. In Jesus name I pray.

"Fear not, for I am with you;
Be not dismayed, for I am your God.
I will strengthen you,
Yes, I will help you,
I will uphold you with My righteous right hand."
~Isaiah 41:10

Why is it that even when He tells us to "fear not" we still fear? When He tells us "Be not dismayed" we distress anyway? It is this flesh's first inclination to fear and distress even knowing the He is our God. If you are the one, that has struggled with fear in this marriage journey-because you suffer insecurities about your worth- I say this to you woman of God, your Father in heaven has for you a man who will show you your worth, and will help you see how the Father in heaven sees you. If you are the one, who has been married before but it didn't work out and fear is keeping you from trying again, I say this to you woman of God repent for whatever may have been fault of yours and this time trust God to send who He made for you- this time it will be different with God at the helm of the ship. If you are the one who has children, and have been a single mother for so long, and are too afraid to speak your desire for marriage to God-He already knows. I say this to you woman of God. The time to carry this burden alone is coming to an end and your Father in Heaven has relief on the way and a strong covering who will become a father to your children. If you are the one who thinks that your past is too messy and your past sin too shameful that no man could possibly want you, I say this to you woman of God. Your past sin has been thrown into the sea of forgetfulness and put under the blood of Jesus. The devil is a liar and God has a husband for you as well. Our husbands need us just as much as we need them don't let satan steal that truth from you. If God is your God like He is mine then know that our fleshly fears are trivial compared to His grandness and power. He tells us not to distress because He is our God. If our thoughts and our will are aligned with His then there will be no need to distress over the unexpected. When He promises to uphold us with His righteous right hand, He is telling us that strength; stability; and assurance are ours. We don't need to fear in this waiting season. We need to trust God at His word. Know that although moments of distress may come, we cannot do as that saying says "die on that hill." We need to allow God to uphold us, with His righteous right hand and not let our past drag us down.

The written word of God says in John 14:9 that Jesus spoke saying, "He who has seen me has seen the Father." In Malachai 3:6 it speaks about God's unchanging nature saying, "He is God, and He changes not." This is written evidence of His unchanging nature and still there are moments where we forget. Because He is the same yesterday, today and forever we can have a guarantee that whatever He speaks or does is eternal and everlasting. We can continually be reassured. Although Jesus carried both man and God within himself, His core nature is still unchanging. Remember when moving in relationships, people change-sometimes for the better and sometimes in not such great ways. Begin to go before Jesus now and gain understanding on the changes that a couple goes through in marriage. It won't always be the honeymoon stage. If you are unprepared, it might be more challenging than if you had some wisdom and impartation from, He who changes not, beforehand. Expect your husband to change, even though at the core of who he is-in the ways that matter the most-he may remain the same. Some things are worth letting go or turning a blind to if it doesn't cause long term impact. Like putting the toilet seat down or leaving their socks on the floor. Even in familial relationships, and friendships seek God's discernment. Some relationships come to an end because God prunes people out of our life if they are not adding or helping us reach purpose, but when it comes to marriage its different. When the changes come too fast or are too much to handle run to God who changes not. He will be there waiting to hear you and offer you direction. Remember He is always your SOURCE.

Patience
&
Preserverance

"But let patience have its perfect work, that you may be perfect and complete, lacking nothing."
~James 1:4

Every process in our li takes patience. Anything taken on and done quickly is never adequately done. Even as I sit writing this devotional, I think about all the times I wanted to quit during the process, because I didn't have the patience to see it through, but God had other plans. While I wanted to write ten devotionals a day, He has only let me do about three and then edit them the same day. Some days I don't even have any words to put on the paper. All through this process I have had to let go of myself and let Him put the words to paper. My prayer has been "Lord All of you and none of me." My desire is that every word be from the mouth of God Himself and from the very throne room of heaven. In this case I have had to let patience have its perfect work. Worship music playing in the background, ministering to me as I work. The Words He places on my heart to put on the pages ministering to me as well in my own season of waiting. He has called me to pull deep from the well within me. By the time this labor of love is completed it will be a perfect and complete work lacking nothing and so will you be. In this waiting learn who you are before you put yourself into the hands of the one God has made for you, so you never feel that you've lost yourself. Your identity is in God Himself not a husband. In this waiting season let patience have its perfect work in you; in your walk with God; in your relationship with Jesus; in your calling and the leading of Holy Spirit, but also in the husband God has for you-he needs a perfect work completed in him as well. You can't do it, only God can. Is there something you feel and know that God has called you to do but you hesitate to do because you lack the patience? Do it. Do it now. In the waiting it's the perfect timing. When the work is complete, and God brings it all together it will lack nothing.

"And not only that, but we also glory in tribulations, knowing that tribulation produces perseverance; and perseverance, character; and character, hope. Now hope does not disappoint, because the love of God has been poured out in our hearts by the Holy Spirit who was given to us."
~Romans 5:3-5

Let's take a minute and be real. Do you glory in tribulations? I know that I should and sometimes I can endure but most of the time with me its "God but what have I done to deserve this," forgetting that simply being His child brings tribulation and persecution. In all honesty I have no clue how my character has become Christ like because I don't do perseverance well. Usually with a face blotchy from crying, eye liner running down my face and voice hoarse from crying out. I know it sounds dramatic but I'm sure there is a little bit of drama queen in all of us at some point in this journey. Even with those drama queen moments, when I snap out of them, I realize that even then I have persevered, and my character has shifted for the better. I can hold on a little longer; I can remind the enemy he is messing with the wrong one; I can say Lord my hope is in you; I can see the bright future God has promised me; I can have the strength to continue in the fight when my flesh says "let's throw in the towel I've had enough." In marriage there will be moments that will feel like you are in the trenches, and throwing in the towel is not the answer. You can't just walk away, and quitting is not the answer. When I was previously married, I was in the trenches, but I kept fighting and fighting, being the Godly standard in our home but because we were unequally yoked-he wanted nothing to do with God-one of us in the fight wasn't enough. At the time I felt like a failure until God gave me the answer I needed to heal. Now I'm waiting on God's choice. During the process I learned to persevere, I learned to hope even when my eyes could not see. Hope never disappointed me even when things did not work out because the love of God poured into me in a way I had never experienced before in my life, and the Holy Spirit comforted me. Holy Spirit heals the deepest wounds if you allow Him to. In your marriage when trials and tribulations come may your heart cry be Lord! I take glory in this season of trial and tribulation if it brings me to a state of perseverance, and the perseverance molds my character into your image, and because my character has been remolded that hope now abides in me as your Holy Spirit abides in me, and is a constant reminder of your love poured out in my heart. In Jesus name I pray Amen.

"And let us not grow weary while doing good, for in due
season we shall reap if we do not lose heart."
~ Galatians 6:9

Discouragement is real. It is one of the biggest tactics of the
enemy of our soul. How does he use discouragement? His
first steps are to make us weary with distractions, like
fighting our thoughts and emotions which are a targeted
type of psychological spiritual warfare. Then He starts on
our identity. He wants to separate us from our Identity in
Christ and get us to Focus on the Identity of our flesh in
order to cause enmity between us and God. If he is
successful in separating us from our identity in Christ, then
he comes with discouragement. Discouragement is real and
it is a hard battle to fight if your feet are not on the firm
foundation that is Jesus Christ. Times come and times go
when we find ourselves lending a hand, or prayer and
support to the people around us, pouring love out until we
feel empty and as if we have nothing else to give and then
weariness comes in like a flood. Why? Because it does not
get reciprocated. I've had times where my prayer has
literally been, "Lord I'm pouring out love left and right but
who is pouring into me?" This is one of the hardest parts
that I have encountered in the season of singleness and
waiting. Pouring out until I feel completely empty and
having no one to pour back into me. One thing I am looking
forward to in marriage is the ability to pour into my
husband and have him pour into me as well. One way to
defeat the enemy's plan and avoid extreme bouts of
weariness while doing good is by not taking up every
opportunity to do good. What I mean by that is this. Just
because you see something needs done doesn't mean just do
it. There are times that we take on burdens that are not
meant to be ours, and this opens doors to negative
emotions. I myself, have a hard time saying No. I always
say yes and then find myself feeling frustrated and short

tempered. I've learned to go before God and ask Him if He wants my yes or my no in different situations. I've also learned to set boundaries. We need to be intentional about not opening doors to give satan access. When you see an opportunity ask God if that opportunity is for you or if it's meant for another laborer. Now if you are doing good, in the will of God, you will notice that you will feel peaceful; you'll feel joy; you'll even find yourself rejoicing which will combat any weariness. The word of God promises that "in due season we will reap if we do not lose heart," the enemy wants to stop you from reaping everything God has for you. Do not let him win when God has already called you victorious.

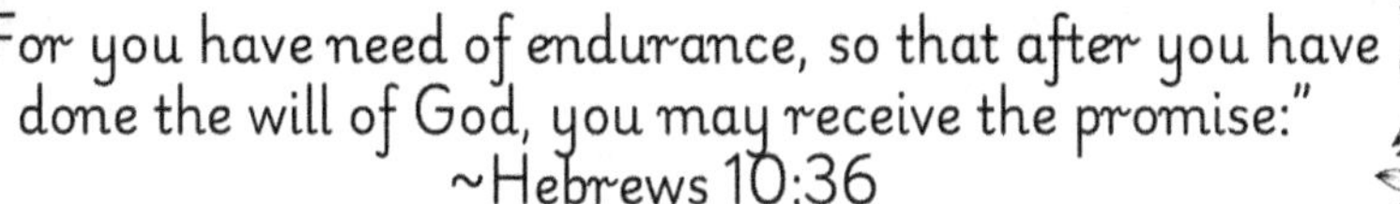

"For you have need of endurance, so that after you have done the will of God, you may receive the promise:"
~Hebrews 10:36

Have you ever asked yourself, if you are a person of endurance? Think of the seasons you have been in the past. Have you endured, "so that after you have done the will of God," you have received the promise? To endure is to last in the face of fatigue, stress or challenges. To endure is to withstand pain or suffering over a long period of time. The issue with today's generation and today's society is that there is no drive to endure. There is no "get up and keep going" mentality like in days past. In the Old Testament the children of Israel endured at times because of persecution and other times because of their choices. In the New Testament Jesus endured because He had a purpose to fulfill. The disciples endured for the cause and to bring others the truth of the word of God. Seasons of waiting are a type of spiritual endurance training. Think about it. In the waiting for your marriage promise, if you allow, God will give you endurance training. He will teach you how to sustain your marriage in the good and the bad. He will teach you how to go on in the face of challenges. He will teach you how to respond and not react in moments of stress. He will teach you how to give even when you are weary and think you don't have it in you, or you need to be poured into; but your spouse isn't there to do it or may even be unwilling to do it. He will teach you to endure when your divine purpose takes every bit of who you are and more but then! "After you have done the will of God." The will of God in seasons of waiting are for you to grow closer to Him and build endurance. Once you've done and learned these things it tells us in the word, "you may receive the promise."

When we wait for the Lord, we are showing Him that we desire above everything for Him to show up in our circumstance or situation and act in whatever way necessary. When we wait, we are giving Him time and allowing Him to work things out to His perfect completion. When we get ahead of Him and rush things or tell Him with our actions that we prefer our plans to His, is where things start to fall apart. In all things wait for the Lord. God will not go against our will. He will do all that we allow Him to do in our lives. He gave us free will, which in reality only brings true freedom when we choose Him above all else. In an article written by Pastor Don Leavell he writes, "waiting on the Lord is one of the most difficult tasks a child of God will ever do. Waiting punishes the natural mind, breaks down the human will, and strains our emotions. However, waiting in faith produces godly results." The answer to our waiting seasons is simple and found in Isaiah 64:4.

"For since the beginning of the world
Men have not heard nor perceived by the ear,
Nor has the eye seen any God besides You,
Who acts for the one who waits for Him."

Know that because you wait, He acts. Even as hard as it is at times, do it without grumbling-I'm talking to myself here too- because He is acting on our behalf. Our waiting though it punishes our natural mind it moves our Lord to action. The breaking of our human will allows us to take on the will of God. The straining of our emotions teaches us to follow what the word of God says and the discernment of Holy Spirit, rather than the heart-which the word describes as deceitful. Emotions are not a bad thing, but they can be deceitful if they rule us rather than we ruling them. Our soul waits because it belongs to Him and recognizes that He is our source. Waiting is not just about trust it is about dependency on God and His power and authority. In His written word there is hope for every emotion, every trial, every challenge, every attack, every season, every valley and every mountain. Hope is the answer to everything under the sun because our hope is Jesus, and Jesus is always the answer.

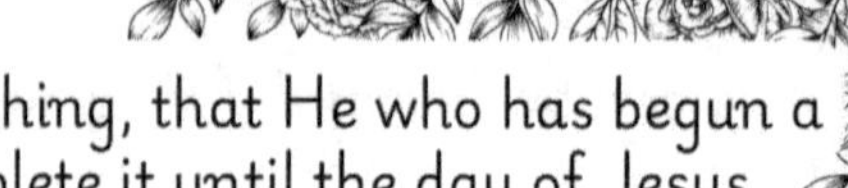

"Being confident of this very thing, that He who has begun a good work in you will complete it until the day of Jesus Christ;"
~Philipians 1:6

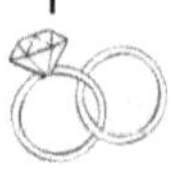

Father God,
You are truly a wonderful and exceeding Father. Thank you because the good work you began from the moment you created me, you will effectively and continually complete until Jesus's anticipated return. Thank you for every season of waiting, where you strip back my layers like an onion, and reveal hidden things inside of me that require healing; submission; repentance and breakthrough, so that the good work you began can continue its path to completion. Elohim thank you because you take my broken pieces and turn them into something and someone beautiful. Thank you, Father, because in the waiting you are also doing a good work in the husband you have chosen. You are consecrating him; leading him back to you; giving him purpose and instruction; purifying him; teaching him how to be a covering over me; teaching him that softness and vulnerability are not weaknesses but strengths within a marriage. Your good work includes molding both of us into the perfect fit for the other, this does not mean we will be perfect people but rather the perfect fit to one another with Jesus at the center gluing us together. Jesus the supernatural super glue. Father you know what you are about, nobody is greater at covenant relationships and covenant promises like you. You are the best and only matchmaker. I relinquish to you my choice and accept your will. Thank you for your good and perfect will in my life and that of my God ordained spouse. In Jesus mighty name. Amen.

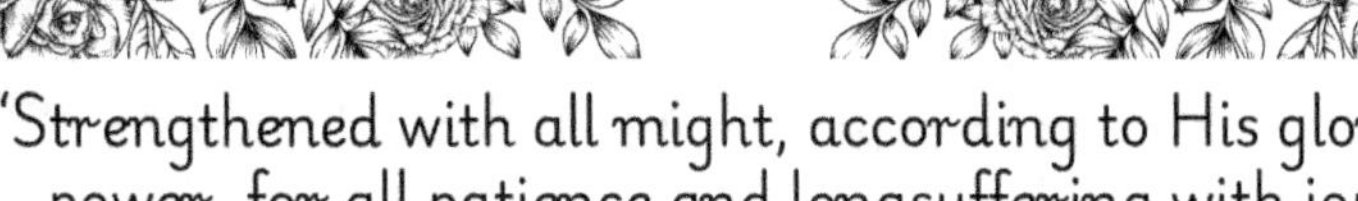

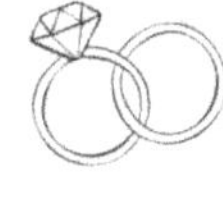

In and of ourselves, we are powerless. Without Father God on the throne and Jesus our High Priest-who makes intercession for us-we would remain powerless. Because of the indwelling of Holy Spirit in us that glorious power flows through us, strengthening us with all might. Our relationship with God is a partnership. He is the ultimate gentleman. He abides in us but He will not go against our will. It is a give and take. He will take everything we surrender turn it into beauty and hand it back or give us better. He takes our stress and gives us patience. He takes our longsuffering and makes it more endurable by giving us joy through that valley or season. Some of us go to the lengths that we exhaust ourselves trying to go it alone before we allow Him to step in and come alongside us. Marriage is a partnership also. If we cannot come together with our husbands, with Jesus at the center strengthening our bond and partnership according to "His glorious power," how can we expect to thrive and not just survive. I don't know about you, but I know that I want my marriage to do more than just survive. I want it to thrive, to grow, to bless, and to be fruitful. I want to partner with my spouse like I partner with God, moving in the same direction and for the same purpose instead of causing strife and division trying to do it on my own or going my own way. Remember that it is written that two shall become one. Unity is always the goal and the standard.

"And do not be conformed to this world, but be transformed by the renewing of your mind, that you may prove what is that good and acceptable and perfect will of God."
~Romans 12:2

There is only one way by which we can be transformed and that is by the renewing of our mind. There is only one way by which we can renew our mind and that is by the word of God- which is His written word. Allot of times we can be misled by thinking that a word spoken over our lives will also transform our lives but that is not the case. A word spoken over our lives will Give us hope, clarity, and direction but the word of God is the only thing that will renew and therefore transform us. Think of a butterfly. It is at first a caterpillar. You can speak to the caterpillar and tell it that it was meant to be a butterfly and it's time for it to transition and transform, but if it does not wrap itself into the cocoon, it will never transform. The cocoon is the vessel by which transformation occurs. When the appointed cycle of transformation is complete, what entered is not what emerges. During the cycle what previously existed, was shed and what was meant to be burst forth, beautiful, majestic, new. We were born into this world, we live in this world, but we cannot allow ourselves to follow the traditions of this world, because this world is not our own. Have you ever heard anyone say, "If you hang out with that person long enough you will begin to act like them" or "if you live in that town long enough, you'll start to drink the same Kool-Aid"? By renewing our minds and therefore transforming into who God designed us to be we are maintaining ourselves apart from becoming part of the fleshly traditions of this world. We are also able to be the light He called us to be and in doing so we are proving to those left in darkness the goodness of God, and His perfect and acceptable will. Lets

go back to the transformation of a caterpillar to a butterfly. As a caterpillar it could only consume, and consume, and consume. Without the cocoon, its vessel of transformation, it would have never become the butterfly. The butterfly was destined to carry the "transference" necessary for flowers to be fertilized and then reproduce. They stop to eat from the flowers and when they move on, they don't leave empty handed. They carry something essential. Renewing your mind and transforming is the only way to learn the essence of what you carry. Do not be conformed, be transformed. Once you learn the essence of what you carry, then you learn to utilize it going forward in your daily life, in your familial and marital relationships, in every encounter. Not a seed of what God has placed in you will be wasted. Do not be conformed, be transformed. Be transformed into the one God requires you to be and the one your husband needs you to become.

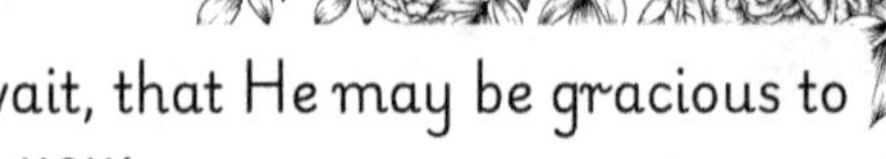

"Therefore the Lord will wait, that He may be gracious to you;
And therefore He will be exalted, that He may have mercy on you.
For the Lord is a God of justice;
Blessed are all those who wait for Him."
~Isaiah 30:18

We are not the only ones that experience waiting. The Lord waits also. He waits for us to act in obedience to His instruction or direction. He waits on His appointed times to arrive. He waits for us to open doors and allow Him access not only to our lives, but also our hearts, our minds, and our decisions. He waits for us to return to Him after we have gone astray. He waits for us to seek Him and acknowledge Him. How does He wait? He waits both diligently and patiently. Why does He wait? So that He may be gracious to us. The Lord's grace is truly a beautiful, unselfish thing. The Lord desires to extend to us His favor and His kindness and so He waits. Not in anger and impatience, not in frustration and condemnation, but with expectation. Scripture tells us that the Lord will be exalted- Lifted and glorified- that He may have mercy on us. When we seek for the Lord's grace in ALL things He will rise with compassion, forgiveness and eagerness in response. The Lord is the God of righteousness; He is committed to upholding truth even when we mess up and believe on a certain level that we have failed Him. In this season recognize and come to the understanding, that because we wait on Him, we are blessed. It is a guarantee Waiting on the Lord is an opportunity to build patience and our dependency on God's timing. If we make the choice to trust His promises, we will come to know His favor and blessings in our life.

God's Love
&
Purpose

"The Lord your God in your midst,
The Mighty One, will save;
He will rejoice over you with gladness,
He will quiet you with His love,
He will rejoice over you with singing."
~Zephaniah 3:17

This verse is a beautiful template of who God is as a father; the redeeming qualities of His son Jesus, whom God has asa stand in spiritual husband until the man he has for you is ready. I don't know about you, but when I pray I tell God that I want Him in the midst of the union between the husband He chose and I. I don't want His presence to come and go. I want it to be a constant never ending, always leading presence. I don't know what you have prayed to God about your husband but I can say that I want the man that was chosen for me to rejoice over me with gladness, to see me as his treasure. I want to rejoice over him with gladness in return. I want to rejoice over him because although it was God's will to bring the two of us together- he still chose to align himself with God's will which deserves to be celebrated. I want that man's love to quiet me in my highs and lows alike. Quiet me like the peace that comes from your favorite blanket or your coziest sweater. I want to do the same for him. I want to let my love speak in the storms of his life and bring the quiet and peace he needs in order to find God again; hear the Lord's voice clearer; or find his way again if he has lost it. I want my love to quiet him like a port in a storm or the anchor that keeps him steady as the waves rock him around. One of my greatest desires and prayers has been for him to be a worshiper, I want to hear that man sing to God standing alongside me. I want him to sing over me the way that I will sing over him- the way that I sing over my children. Because man is indeed made in the image of God- of which I have no doubt- then I know that all of this is not impossible for God.

The Bible says that we are fearfully and wonderfully made. What does that truly mean? It means that the God that created us knows us intimately, even from the moment He formed us in the womb. It means that He knows every detail about us. We are His workmanship therefore we are marvelous in His sight. Think about the God sent spouse that's on his way to finding you for a minute. As intimately as the Lord knows you, His creation, what are some of the characteristics that you think he will carry? You must know yourself as intimately as the Lord knows you. Have you ever self examined yourself and intimately discovered things that you just didn't want to face? I'm not talking about the physical. I'm speaking about soul deep. I'm talking about buried scars in your psyche. I've been there and it is not pretty, but He gives you the strength to face it all. Despite this the Lord says that marvelous are His works, that includes you. That also includes the husband you are waiting for. When you pray for this man, declare "I Praise you Lord, for he(husband) is fearfully and wonderfully made; marvelous are your works, and that my soul knows very well". God knows him intimately more than you ever will. The Lord knows his courage and hesitations. The Lord knows his fears and his strengths. He knows his power and his weakness. The Lord formed him in the womb and placed in him the intimacy required to help you face those things that you discovered that you don't want to face alone. You will also help him overcome his scars with peace, acceptance, love. If our soul knows very well that marvelous are His works, than we can trust the time it will take to get us and them to be ready for one another. God does not work in microwave timers, He operates on His timing.

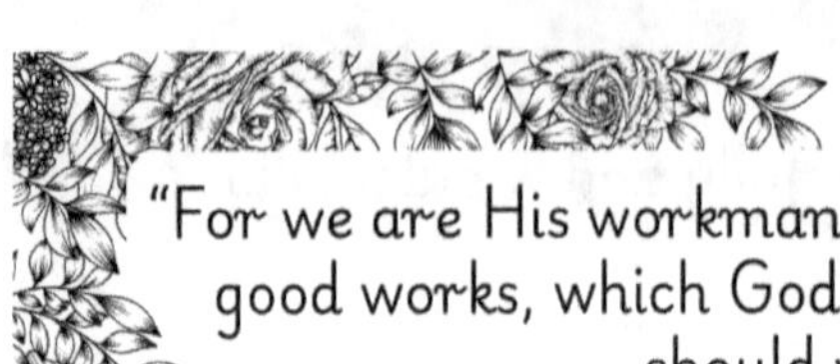

"For we are His workmanship, created in Christ Jesus for good works, which God prepared beforehand that we should walk in them."
~Ephesians 2:10

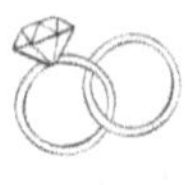

If you didn't know it before workmanship translates to work in progress. Have you ever seen those door hang signs that say testing in progress? With complete transparency here, sometimes it feels like I have a sign hanging around my neck announcing that I am a work in progress. Have you ever felt the same way? In our flesh it can be frustrating to believe and feel that we have acquired the necessary transformation in a specific season only to realize Father God is saying through the Holy Spirit "not yet"; "You're still holding back on me"; "you're not letting go of that self righteousness"; "you're fear won't let you lay that on the altar"; if you don't let me touch that issue I can't heal you"; "you have not surrendered completely"; "You're condemning yourself." None of those things in reality are things that we want to hear. Sometimes we want to hold on to our "junk" (think Linus from Charlie Brown, forever dragging his blanket behind him) and use it as a defense mechanism or a shield. Please know that you have never been an after thought to God. He prepared the good work of your future marriage with foresight. Your marriage will require your best, it will take the both of you with God at the center, but because of His foresight He already prepared the way and all you have to do is walk it out.

Lord thank you for loving me even when I was unlovable. Thank you for loving me when I was invisible to everyone around me but never you. Lord thank you for your grace that has made me worthy of your love. Thank you because the precious blood of your son Jesus covers my sin and brings me into your sight. Lord I love you because you Love me. I love you because you have shown me that Love requires action, and every action you've taken in my life has spoken the love you have for me out loud. I love you because you have redeemed me with an everlasting love. I love you because when everyone has left me you have remained by my side as master, Father, savior, friend. Thank you Lord for showing me that your love is worth every sacrifice. In Jesus name I pray. Amen

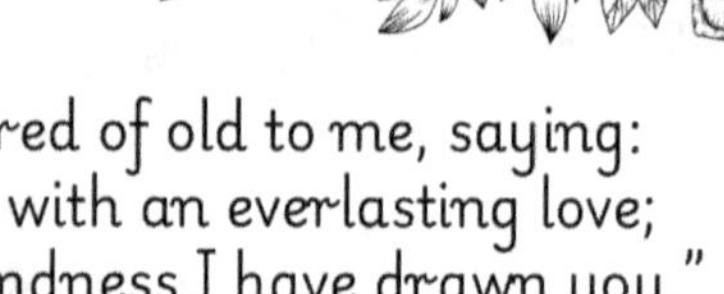

"The Lord has appeared of old to me, saying:
"Yes, I have loved you with an everlasting love;
Therefore with lovingkindness I have drawn you."
~Jeremiah 31:3

The Lord's love is what draws us to Him. Once we are drawn to Him who is love itself, then His love should abide in us. Have you ever noticed that there are seasons in your life where every time you turn around, it's as if people are drawing near to you, that is the love of God in you wooing them in. Be aware not all of them have good intentions, use discernment. Our value is not dependent on our relationship status, but rather on God's steadfast everlasting love. God's love is a source of present fulfillment, not a reason to feel incomplete. God's faithfulness is a source of hope that we have not been forgotten. His faithfulness is constant and draws us to Him with loving-kindness even through uncertainty and trepidation. Instead of focusing on finding that special partner focus on becoming the "good thing" God wants you to be. By becoming whole and healed in God you will be more prepared to be a partner in a healthy godly marriage when the time is right.

Faith
&
Encouragement

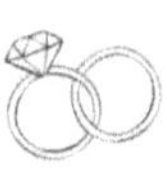

When I think of substance, I think of something tangible;
able to be held in hand or seen with the eyes but that's not
how it works in the ways of God. When you look at this
verse at first it almost sounds contradictory. How can faith
be a substance of hope? How can faith be the evidence of
things not seen? While reading to attempt to answer these
questions for both myself and all of you I came across the
following: "Faith acts as a "spiritual eyesight". It allows a
person to be as certain of invisible truths as they are of the
physical world around them, leading them to act based on
those unseen realities." I believe that is the closest we will get
to answering those questions. Unless some of you already
had this revelation previously. During a period of waiting,
faith is not just a hopeful wish, but an active confidence in
God's promise for marriage and a conviction in His unseen
plan. Hope can feel so empty when the desired outcome is
delayed. Hope is grounded in the belief in God's promises
and His character not just our own wishes. Ever heard that
expression "if wishes were horses beggars would ride?" If we
could simply reach our goals and promises by wishing for
them everything would be easy, but we are not called to
wish but to believe. You may not see your future spouse or
your future life together but faith provides the "assurance"
in what you are hoping for and conviction about what you
do not see. Trusting God has a plan even when it is not yet
visible. Waiting is an exercise in yielding control to God's
timeline rather than our own. Anyone else have trouble
yielding control? I want to jump up and down shouting, me,
me, me. Sigh. I don't want control because I believe I can do
it faster or better than God. I don't think that way. I don't

want to control because I want it right now and need to have it right now. I have trouble at times yielding control because I fear the unknown, even though I trust and believe what the Lord has said. Sometimes the unknown to me is like a black hole waiting to suck you in. Anyone else ever feel like that or is it just me? I literally have to visualize Jesus standing in place of the black hole in order to yield control. I am a work in progress, God's workmanship who has struggles and is imperfect. I am by no means an expert. I have just been vulnerable in this journey with you, placing on these pages the words the Holy Spirit has placed in my heart for all of us, added with a little spice of my personality. Joking about the spice of my personality. It is an active choice to trust in God's promises throughout the journey, especially when facing uncertainty doubt or disappointment.

"And whatever things you ask in prayer, believing, you will receive."
~Matthew 21:22

"Therefore I say to you, whatever things you ask when you pray, believe that you receive them, and you will have them."
~Mark 11:24

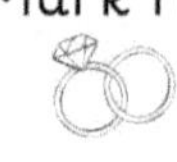

When you pray, pray that God gives you the character and readiness for marriage. Sometimes we beg God in prayer for what we want -the marriage-but forget to ask Him to change us in the process. There must be a shift in our characters. God is not going to make a way for marriage if we are not willing to submit to His refinement and remolding process. It has to be a sacrificial act. Asking in prayer is not a demand. God DOES NOT respond to demands, especially not for a spouse on a personal timeline. We need to actively believe God will answer prayers that align with His will, even as He works on preparing us internally. Pray for that spouse with the belief that you will receive one when it is aligned with God's will. When you pray say to Him, "Lord How do you want me to pray, because I want to pray your will not my will." If you don't receive a direction then pray in the spirit and allow the Holy Spirit to help you intercede. Encourage yourself to have faith in God's plan. God is working not just to shape our character, but He is also working to shape our heart, heal past wounds-He doesn't just want to cauterize them to stop the pain He wants to Heal them-build your capacity for a healthy marriage. Let us use this time to pray for the qualities needed for a strong marriage, allowing God to correct any misconceptions that we may have. Pray for patience, contentment, strength and a deeper understanding of God's will. Ask the Holy Spirit to bind your mouth from speaking words of fear and frustration and to help you speak words that give life. Marl 11:24 is not just about the final outcome but about being ready for it. When God's timing arrives you will be prepared to embrace it. While waiting seek to be satisfied and complete in God, rather than in a person. This helps you avoid settling for the wrong person out of impatience. Trust that God will provide what is best even if it is different from what is initially expected. Let go of expectations. He is Jehova Jireh our provider, of course He provides the best for His children. Let go of expectations. Our focus should always be what God wills for our life, as He has a perfect plan that is ultimately the best in every way. Use this waiting season to invest in yourself. Try things like reading, learning, gaining new skills, start a business, become more self sufficient, and a better partner for the future. Don't run into relationships out of emotion, but at the same time don't hold back out of fear. Waiting can help you avoid making mistakes-like marrying the wrong person due to impatience-and helps you go to God seeking His face and getting the green light.

Outer strength and honor are often reflections of inner growth rather than just appearance. Clothing ourselves in strength and dignity means developing strong faith, living with purpose and being wise in our choices. This prepares us for the future by building a foundation of resilience and character, so that marriage can be met while already living a purposeful life not by simply waiting for one to start. Waiting seasons are definitely a test in making wise choices. Our flesh wants to rise up again and again, it wants to walk away and give up, it wants what it wants when it wants, it wants to purposely misunderstand the situations in order to self justify rebellion. Every time we battle our flesh and get it into submission we put another stone on that foundation of resilience and character. Clothing ourselves in strength and dignity is also about building a strong spiritual foundation built on faith and wisdom. If we are prepared and secure in our identity and trusting completely in God's plan then we will live with a lack of fear. Let me lay this "warning" right here. Don't make marriage your sole ambition, instead focus on the assignment God has for you now, because If you do you will sadly find yourself unfulfilled. Be purposeful. A woman with a life of direction, that allows God to be her compass. A woman whose passion and purpose is attractive. A woman that makes a mission driven life her focus. Focus on being the woman you were created to be and you will rejoice at your appointed time.

I'm coming to the conclusion that we can learn allot from the blind about faith. The blind have to rely on heightened sensory attunement to navigate daily life and maintain independence, as well as other things. The blind don't have what one would consider "super powers" but they rely more heavily on their other senses, leading to greater attunement and neurological adaptation. Hearing, touch and smell are what they use to navigate life. They use hearing to identify traffic patterns, recognize voices, and utilize echolocation to detect the distance and size of obstacles. Imagine if we listened with our spiritual ears and not just what our flesh speaks to us. The Bible says that "faith comes from hearing and hearing by the word of God". The Bible also says "My sheep recognize my voice and the voice of the enemy they do not follow." Why aren't we listening? Or are we listening but to the wrong voice. We are listening to Fear, the tactic of the enemy. They use touch essential for reading Braille, feeling changes in terrain through the feet, and identifying objects by texture or shape. When the woman with the issue of blood made her way through the crowd and touched just the hem of Jesus garment she was immediately healed . Her faith touched Him and He immediately said "who touched me" Jesus knew it was not the brush of the crowd bumping against him, but an intentional touch that had virtue flowing out of Him. Dunamis is the Greek word for virtue in Luke 8:36, meaning miraculous power. There are times you just have to reach out and touch Jesus anyway way you can through this journey of waiting. The woman with the issue reached, crawled pressed in through the crowd because she just had to get to Jesus. Have there been moments on this journey you felt you had to press in deeper but you gave up just before the breakthrough? Press in until you feel the miraculous power of God move through you and make a way when you thought there was no way. The children of God know when they have been touched by their savior and Lord. The touch of God is like no other feeling you will ever experience in your life, it does not ever leave you the same. We can Identify the Lord by His touch on our lives in our hearts in our thought patterns. When Moses came down from the mountain he had to cover himself because the glory of God was on him and if anyone looked upon it they would fall dead. May we come down from the presence of God so changed that anyone who encounters us may die to their sin immediately and leave changed from the presence of God in us and on us. Every time you leave the presence of God you should be leaving changed. The blind use smell for environmental cues and determining the freshness of food. Have you ever been in a church service and all of a sudden the sweetest smell enters the atmosphere and you know the presence of God has entered the room. Have you ever experienced it in the privacy of your own home? Its the environmental cue that you are entertaining the supernatural and its meeting your natural. During this time of walking by faith and not by sight, focus on growing in areas like emotional wisdom and communication as marriage will magnify any existing issues. Plan and prepare for your future marriage by creating a blueprint for a God fearing home and identifying areas for personal improvement. Walking by faith means taking steps of faith while trusting God to provide the next part of the plan. For example prepare yourself, make a plan and trust Him to provide the means like financial provision or the right person.

"And those who know Your name will put their trust in You;
For You, Lord, have not forsaken those who seek You."
~Psalm 9:10

What is the value of a name? In Hebrew culture it is believed to be the essence of a person, a reflection of their soul, and a potential map for their life's mission. Parents are said to have experienced, intuitively choosing a name that aligns with that child's future character and destiny. We see in the scriptures that God places importance on names. He changed the name of Abram and Sarai. He gave the name to John, Samson and Jesus. All went on to do miraculous things but most notable was our Lord Jesus, who the bible speaks of and declares that "His name is the name above every name and that there is no other name by which we might be saved." I say this so that you can see that His name speaks His character, and His character says He is not a Forsaker of His people. That revelation right there should lead you to shout in praise. All over the scriptures He showed up again and again for His children and His people. Even in their disobedience He never forsook them and He will never forsake you. Waiting seasons are not times of uncertainty, but opportunities to learn His character. God is a faithful stronghold who will not abandon us if we are faithful to seek Him. We have to give up our own understanding and desires for a partner, its a necessity and let His will be the way. The Lord will not leave you to face your future alone. This next statement I know to be true in my own life. Seasons of waiting are often used by God to strip away other dependencies, showing us that He alone is truly sufficient to meet our needs and longings. I will tell you, that when I submitted my life again as an adult and started truly living for Him, I could not go anywhere without receiving a prophetic word over my life. I got so used to it. I got used to going to my closest mentors when I

needed clarity on something God was showing me and telling me that I stopped depending on Him and hearing what He had to say and hearing His direction. That was a MAJOR mistake. Now in this season He has given me no other voice but His to listen to and depend on. All my mentors have been moved out of my circle dealing with life issues and changes that I cannot go to them anymore. I have no more prophetic words chasing me down at every corner. At the beginning I felt as if God had abandoned me, or as if all the air had been sucked out of the room. Let me tell you I struggled. I cried. I felt anger and frustration. It was ugly at first, but then I understood. Every voice became louder than His voice so He had to silence them all. Patience comes from knowing God. Knowing God gives us the confidence to wait patiently for the right person, rather than settling out of fear or desperation. It comes from the knowledge of God's character and your trust in His plans for you. He won't forsake you or His promises and plans for your life. You can trust His timing and His choice of a future Spouse.

"For I, the Lord your God, will hold your right hand,
Saying to you, 'Fear not, I will help you."
~Isaiah 41:13

I think there are times a person can take God's help for granted. It can be as simple as failing to thank Him, and show Him how much we appreciate His help. It can be allowing our request to become demands and treating His help like an obligation. We can easily treat Him like He owes us something instead of us owing Him everything. We become frustrated or angry if God stays silent when we are begging Him for answers it's not time for Him to answer. Feeling like we have been denied something we believe we deserve as His children. It is a straight and narrow walk and a balancing act. This scripture is a guarantee of God's presence, guidance and help. It is an encouragement to trust His timing and not be afraid of the delays that we encounter. In case you need to hear this, God is not just sitting around on His throne during our waiting season doing nothing. He is actively involved in every part of it. Try to visualize Him holding your hand and leading you. This verse is a constant assurance that God is physically present, which can bring you relief to your feelings of loneliness or powerlessness. The purpose of waiting is not to be inactive. We must use the time to get our lives in order and make room for what is on it's way. It cannot arrive if there is no place for it. Use the time wisely. We know that there is nothing about God that is random. You better believe that His timing is not random either but purposeful and intentional and ultimately it will lead to a better outcome than we could have ever imagined. Keep your focus and stay rooted in scripture, pray honestly about your feelings. Are you having trouble praying honestly about your feelings to your Heavenly Father? Let me tell you that there are times when I have trouble. Its like "God you don't need to hear my pitiful feelings when there are bigger problems in the world," but let me tell you, He is your daddy and already knows your heart and He just wants to hear you have the confidence to come talk to Him about it. Let me tell you a little story. When I was in fifth grade I had a little crush on a boy named Juan, and I remember one day he broke my heart at recess- well as much as a kid can be heart broken over unrealistic childish love. I remember my dad had stopped in to check on me like he sometimes did at school, make sure I was behaving. This day though I don't think there was anything random about it. I think he sensed that his little girl needed him. Of course the teacher gave him a great report. I asked him if I could come home early, and so he told me yes probably sensing I wasn't alright. When I got in the van the tears I had been holding back came flushing out. I'll tell you, dad was stoic, when he said "Addie what's wrong?" Of course I was not gonna let slip that I'd had a boyfriend, that was spanking territory. All I said was a friend that was a boy didn't want to be my friend anymore. My daddy said to me, "If he doesn't want to be your friend then that means he just wasn't worth your time." I realize my dad knew his stuff and he saw more than I wanted him to see but He was gracious enough not to embarrass me. Our Father in heaven is just the same. He already knows but he wants you to put it all out to Him, and He knows just what to say to comfort you, and He knows exactly what scripture to lead you to in order to uplift you. Find ways to serve faithfully knowing that there is purpose in the present. Pray for guidance on a daily basis and strength and take the time to reflect on God's presence in your life especially difficult moments.

"Peace I leave with you, My peace I give to you; not as the world gives do I give to you. Let not your heart be troubled, neither let it be afraid."
~John 14:27

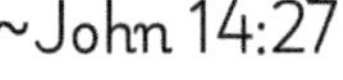

Jesus provides us with a source of internal, divine peace that enables us to trust God's timing instead of the world's, allowing us to focus on spiritual preparation rather than anxiety. Anxiety is real and I'm by no means discounting it, but the less we focus on it and the more we press past it breaking self imposed boundaries the more we overcome it. I've been there but God has delivered me and He can deliver you too. The peace that Jesus offers us is a peace that comes from within and transcendent- coming from a higher power source-not a peace dependent on our external circumstances like the worlds, so that if we search inside of ourselves we can find it even though the wait is hard. This internal, divine peace helps calm the anxiety that comes from wondering the "when" and the "with whom" we will marry. Don't waste this precious time that God has given you, this waiting season is a God given opportunity for spiritual growth, and refinement. Reality is we never stop growing in God. We never stop healing because He continually peels us back like the layers of an onion. He finds the hidden things we didn't even know were there stealing His precious peace from us. Another reality is that refinement is not painless, but it comes with its own benefits, like intimacy with God. Deepen your relationship with God. Strengthen your faith, develop your character into that of a future spouse so that when marriage arrives you don't go through the fire of learning a role you had the

time to prepare for. Focusing on God's will for our life allows us to submit to God's timing in peace, rather than trying to force our own agenda, truly trusting that He is working for our good and our future family. Let us decide today, together, to consciously turn our concerns about marriage over to God through prayer with a spirit of thanksgiving to experience His peace.

"Rejoice always, pray without ceasing, in everything give thanks; for this is the will of God in Christ Jesus for you."
~1Thessalonians 5:16-18

This verse is a call to find your joy so that with rejoicing you can pray without ceasing and give thanks from a pure heart. When I have trouble finding Joy I get in my car and go for a drive windows down feeling the wind in my hair and the sun on my face and I'm able to find my joy again. There are times I go walking on the trail and something as simple as hearing the birds singing or flying across my path sets my heart alight, and I remember how to rejoice in the simple things and I hold on to that feeling. I use those walks to commune with God in a way that does not feel pressured, stilted or hard. I am able to express my gratitude in freedom and with all sincerity and honesty of heart, even in moments where I do not understand His purpose. Even thought I am in a season of waiting I'm also in a season of expressing my gratitude to God because I am walking in His purpose for my life at the same time, putting the gifts He has placed in me to use for His kingdom. Be purposeful, cultivate patience, trust and spiritually mature. Do you know that you are not just waiting on a marriage? You are also waiting on your "partner". The Joy that we find in Christ is a fruit of the Holy Spirit's work in us. Have you ever been going about your day and then something just triggers a fit of giggles and you just can't seem to stop yourself from laughing? That is a touch from God. I love those moments. Every time I see a deer or a cardinal, my cup of joy runs over. I feel like a little girl again. There is just an innocent freedom that children have, before the world and situations intervene, stealing it away. Remember that Jesus overcame the world, even when you feel sad or discouraged. Hearing that when we are going through it should bring comfort, and I understand that sometimes those words don't seem like enough, but get back in your word and read what He endured for us. That will make the words more than words. The words will become your hope for better days and relief. Actively look for the good in your life and find reasons to be joyful despite the current circumstances. Praying without ceasing is something that comes easier to some than others. One reason is because it's easier to bring your cares to a tangible person you can talk face to face to. Another reason-my reason in the past has been because I didn't want to bother God with what I believed to be petty complaints when He is the all important God. My reasons of course were not valid but a deception of the enemy, and a ploy to silence me. When we consistently bring our feelings, struggles and hope to God through prayer it deepens our relationship with Him. Don't just pray for your "partner" but also for patience, wisdom and a stronger faith. Give thanks in all circumstances. Even when we are frustrated by the wait we must make a conscious effort to be thankful for the blessings we already have. Being thankful shifts our focus from what we lack to what we have, it helps keep us from a complaining mindset. How do you think that waiting has helped you build patience, character and faith? Find encouragement in the journey. Connect with trusted friends who can encourage you and pray with you, helping you stay hopeful and preventing feelings of bitterness or disillusionment. Use discernment in choosing the friends. Not everyone will understand your journey and can hinder it unintentionally, instead of helping you. You can also be a source of encouragement for others going through the same experience. You will find joy in encouraging others even when you can't find the strength to encourage yourself.

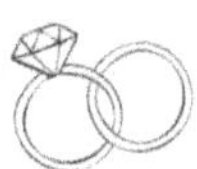

One thing that we can be consistently sure of is that the living word of God provides guidance and clarity. We must make it a necessity to refer back to it for daily decisions, seeking its-tried and true- wisdom for direction and finding hope and comfort in it during this waiting period. A marital relationship closely resembles and models our walk with God. Our walk with God should be a daily devoted relationship, that requires constant and sustained communication, as a way to comprehend His will and build patience. Did I mention I lack patience? Right here there would be the eye roll emoji if it was allowed but since its not lets move on. If you cannot daily devote yourself to God in some way shape or form how will you be able to devote yourself in a marriage. I challenge you to sit with God and make a list. Folded it in half. On one side write all the ways that you show God that you are devoted to Him—not for his sake—so that you can see if there is any area you can make adjustments and deepen your relationship. One the other half—here is the revelatory part- write down all the ways you would like your future husband to show his devotion to you and your marriage. Now here is the sacrificial part. Ask yourself if you are willing to give the same type of devotion that you need or require. If you are, then that is sacrificing self. If you are not then go before God and ask Holy Spirit to help you do the work. To do the work in your relationship with Him and then with the future husband. This is not about failing it's about deepening your spiritual relationship and healing the areas that cause you to hold back. Spend time in the word daily, seek guidance from it; meditate on the scriptures to receive clarity for decisions you need to make immediate or otherwise and to navigate any challenges in the waiting season. No time in the word is ever wasted. I cannot say this enough, believe me I say it myself several times a day, trust in God's plan. Has God's word provided you direction before? Has He provided direction even when the path seems uncertain or feels dark? I know that my answer is yes. Then trust that it will again and again. Patience. Do you find yourself lacking patience? I know I do. I'll be doing great and then impatience sneaks up on me if my guard is not up. I know that I need work in that area. I think that's why God blessed me with a son who has ADHD. Yes he is a blessing in many ways, especially in helping me be patient. I'm not always patient, I struggle with being reactive- must be the Puerto Rican blood- feisty and fiery it is. It forces me to acknowledge that before I respond to his "challenges" I have to pause and not react, before redirecting. Pausing and responding requires patience. You know what else requires patience? It is a crucial component of marriage. When we practice patience with the little things in life we become more prepared for the bigger ones. Make a challenge with yourself to deepen your relationship with God so that it becomes continuous day and night. Deepen your relationship with Him through His word allowing it to be a lamp that guides your feet and a light that illuminates your path. Communicating with God through His word is alike to the communication in marriage. Its practice with added benefit from the Lord.

Hope In God

"May the God of hope fill you with all joy and peace as you trust in him, so that you may overflow with hope by the power of the Holy Spirit."
~Romans 15:13

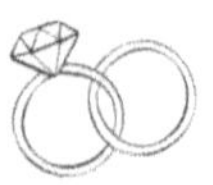

Have you ever looked at your circumstances and wondered how you were going to praise and worship through? Have you tried finding joy and peace in the midst of that situation and could find none to sustain you or lead you though? Joy and peace only come through God's provision. How do you find joy in God's provision? For me the joy comes in the lightness I feel when I put the weight of my burdens into His hands. It's like I can breathe again and the joy and peace saturate me in His presence and provision. How do you actively live out your faith, while expecting future fulfillment? I'm going to be completely open here. I have a prophetic gift. There are times Holy Spirit will give me prophetic acts of faith to do. For example, He had me sit down and make a list of items that the Lord wanted me to buy and put into a groom's chest for my future husband. At first I thought it was "crazy". I'm sure if I had told anyone except for two women of God close to me I would have come under censoring and judgement. Sometimes He will draw you into a Noah experience where people just won't get it but you be obedient to the task at hand. So I go to the store and I buy items that the Holy Spirit shows me and put it in the chest for him. Prophetic acts of faith. I can't see it yet but these seeds of faith are taking root. We have to prioritize who and what we invest our hope in. Instead of placing faith in our future spouses or in our future marriages we should be placing our ultimate hope and faith in God who is the source of all hope and faithful to ALL of His promises. According to the Bible-the living word of God- hope is not just positive

wishing it is a consistent and confident expectation based on God's character and promises. Do not idolize marriage future or present. God is a jealous God. Your hope should not be dependent on getting married. Hope is a gift from God that should overflow regardless of marital status. I think believers forget the importance of the role of the Holy Spirit. We forget that He is a person and an open line of communication between us and God. He is also the one who leads us back to where we need to be when we are drifting away. He also brings to us the provision of God. Actively ask Holy Spirit to empower your hope filling you to the point of overflowing. This type of supernatural hope will sustain you through the wait. Practice active hope. How? Live faithfully daily by walking in the purpose God has given you. Do you know what your purpose is? If you don't that is step one. Serve others, celebrating small blessings while holding onto the promise of fulfillment.

"This hope we have as an anchor of the soul, both sure and steadfast, and which enters the Presence behind the veil,"
~Hebrews 6:19

Have you ever struggled with confidence? I have all my life. When I was a kid I was the girl with the long oval face, teeth too big and skinny as a bean pole- I literally had a bully in the neighborhood who called me "chicken legs" while she clucked at me like a chicken from her third floor window. At home I would walk on egg shells all the time. I had an explosive mother who nothing was ever good enough because I "didn't come out like her". I'm guessing she meant my personality. I had zero confidence, and it was a battle I battled most of my life to overcome. Sometimes that little girl in me still wants to hide or be cautious when I walk into a room but it took Jesus to be able to walk into a room with my head held high, pretending to belong until I did. God is so good. The confidence I gained through that struggle and others; through that feeling of not being worthy; or feeling like I was ever enough, built up over time into a steadfast expectation in God's plan rather than my circumstance. What struggles have you faced that have helped you build up a steadfast expectation in God's plan rather than your circumstances? I sincerely would like to say that my hope in Christ provided a stable foundation to endure delays and disappointment with patience faith and assurance, but I'm not quite there yet. In complete vulnerability during my private time with the Lord this week I came to Him with openness in my prayer and told Him I didn't know how much longer I could wait. I had hope but my hope was lagging, even though I have a history of seeing God work miracles in my life that only He could have done. My foundation was shaking and beginning to show cracks, I wasn't as strong as those around me perceived me to be. In His gentleness He answered with love, "Daughter don't fail me now. Don't fail in your hope. Everything that I've promised is on the way, Hold on just a little longer." When I tell you that the dam broke in my emotions, it was like a flood and the numbness that had entered my spirit drifted away and disappeared. I'm choosing to hold on anchored to Jesus. The delays have felt crushing, the disappointments felt as if I would not recover, patience I have lacked all my life but now I'm in a season of patience building and I have faith even if it's the size of a mustard seed. I have a new assurance from my Father in Heaven. Instead of feeling adrift the hope described in this verse anchors our heart to God. We have to approach hope as a steadfast anchor in our lives during the turbulent and uncertain emotional waters of waiting for a spouse. I believe that there are times when we confuse hope with wishful thinking. Hope is NOT wishful thinking-it is a confident expectation of God's timing and promises. The anchor of hope helps us to maintain our security through the storms of disappointment or confusion that comes along with waiting. Lets be honest, who likes to face disappointment? Nobody. Disappointment at times makes us face ourselves and our roles that could have led to it. Remember that despite current circumstances God is in control and His promises are certain. Anchor your hope in God who is constant and unchanging- He is the I AM- rather than in shifting circumstances.

"Blessed is the man who trusts in the Lord,
And whose hope is the Lord.
For he shall be like a tree planted by the waters,
Which spreads out its roots by the river,
And will not fear when heat comes;
But its leaf will be green,
And will not be anxious in the year of drought,
Nor will cease from yielding fruit."
~Jeremiah 17:7-8

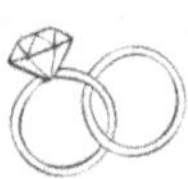

I want to be a tree planted by the waters. I want my trust in the Lord to be everything and my roots so deeply anchored in the river that nothing that comes my way causes me to stumble in fear. I'm still in the stage of my walk with God that instead of completely relying on Him for fulfillment that my default is anxious expectation. We are all a work in progress and I will continue to walk until my steps are more sure in Him and beyond. We have to get to the point in our walk where we completely trust the Lord and rely on him rather than anxious expectation for a relationship. Are you deeply rooted in Him? Or do you desire to be?This season of waiting is the perfect opportunity to draw sustenance and stability directly from God regardless of our external circumstances. It will teach you to stand during your marriage if the need ever arises. Take this time to deepen your personal relationship with God. I would never give up the last five years of waiting for anything. The growth and intimacy with God that I've gained I wouldn't trade for anything. Let us allow our faith to be deeply rooted so that our joy and identity are not dependent on our marriage status. Waiting brings challenges and even emotional droughts sometimes. I have had moments that I have cried until I had no more tears left and felt absolutely numb to everything. That's not depression lets just be clear, its just been a weight that felt too heavy to carry because I tried

carrying it on my own. How deeply you are rooted in God will determine if you will wither or be stable and resilient. True fulfillment and stability comes from the Lord—not from a spouse or marriage. Focus on the source and seek the ultimate satisfaction that is in God alone, which prepares you to enter a future as a whole person whose primary source in life is secure. One thing I am learning is that you cannot live your season of singleness like your life is on hold until marriage. While doing research for this devotional I read that "a tree does not fail to bear fruit." That struck me deep. Make your season of singleness and waiting a fruitful time. Focus on personal growth; serving others; developing skills; and pursuing your purpose. You must flourish where you are planted.

"Why are you cast down, O my soul?
And why are you disquieted within me?
Hope in God;
For I shall yet praise Him,
The help of my countenance and my God."
~Psalm 42:11

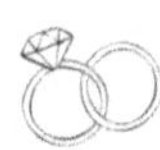

Sometimes you have to speak to your own soul. Other times you have to encourage yourself especially in seasons of despair. This scripture is a cry to reject despair and trust in God and His faithfulness. David the psalmist first tells his soul to "hope in God". Then he professes with unshakable certainty "For I shall yet praise Him," the expectation that deliverance is surely to come as well as another chance to praise God again. Do you ever speak to your soul? Have you felt "cast down" or "disquieted" in this season? It's okay to acknowledge those feelings to yourself and to God. Trusting God's timing is not a one time thing but a choice that we have to make again and again. You have to decide what emotion you are going to feed. Choose to feed hope over despair, even when you don't understand; even through delays and disappointments-because there will be many, Don't let the negative feelings that rise up from your soul to dictate your faith. Do you ever feel that your waiting season has just become this void of negative emotions, trials with negative outcomes, where rebellion just wants to take over? Lets be real, sometimes this flesh and this soul wants to rebel against the plan of God because the wait is more than we were prepared to give, and has just become a drain of our will to stand. Waiting is not a negative void, but purposeful refining faith. The wait and the fight is long and its hard, because what comes with the marriage is not just a partner. The preparation is for the "weight of Glory that comes with marriage". If you give up now, if you let your soul lead the way you'll be giving up the weight of that

Glory. Rushing leads to mistakes, so don't rush the process because the cry of your soul is louder than the promise of God. Look forward to future praise. The praise you have in advance of victory is nothing like the praise that comes when victory has in all actuality been attained. You will have victory over every feeling of discouragement. A time of rejoicing and praise WILL return when you are ready. You chose when to rejoice. You choose when to praise. STOP looking with your eyes and feeling with your soul. Remember that waiting seasons, although for you may be seasons of struggle that all seasons of struggle are temporary including this one. A sacrifice of praise in your current season can change your outlook completely. By praising God for what He has done and for His faithfulness, you can foster a sense of hope even when you don't feel it.

Why is it that we know that we know that the Lord can do everything, yet we doubt Him. Or is it that we doubt that we have heard Him correctly or interpreted what He has shown us correctly? God is sovereign. His timing perfect. His plans for our spouses is unthwartable. He teaches us humility and patience reminding us again that delaying marriage doesn't mean denial, but rather allows God to prepare you and your future partner for His best. It shifts our focus from hurried personal desire. God's will is unfallible. No free will ever supersedes God's will. God's plans are always perfect. Recognize your process. What God is doing in your life is not by accident, it is orchestrated planning. Don't rush your process because God's plans are never delayed, although it may seem so to us He is never late. His plan for our marriage is not limited by OUR timeline or circumstances. His purpose will be fulfilled even if it feels slow. God's plan is to bring the right person at the right time. We need to submit our desires to God's will recognizing that our understanding is limited and His is perfect, leading to a deeper and more prepared union. This verse counters any desperation that may arise within us with hope assuring us that God's plans are for peace a future and a hope not to harm or delay us indefinitely.

"Now to Him who is able to do exceedingly abundantly above all that we ask or think, according to the power that works in us, to Him be glory in the church by Christ Jesus to all generations, forever and ever. Amen."
~Ephesians 3:20-21

The word says that He is able. Have you ever sat down and prayed for something and have the Lord respond saying you aren't dreaming big enough?" I've had that happen. We are limited in our thinking, so it is easy for God to do exceedingly above all that we can ask or think. Here is the kicker, He does these big exceeding things through His power at work in us. One way we use that power is by the words we "choose" to decree and declare, the words we pray. Are you using the power of your words as you wait for that husband to find you. I must confess that I have not matured as much as I would like in this area. I continually fall back on my default of voicing my feelings. Is this your default too? I admit with confidence that I am a work in progress and I am determined to speak only what my faith desires to see happen. We have to come to the realization that if we partner with God He Himself will put the words on our lips to decree a thing so that it is established. We are also a people with limited vision. Has God ever blessed you with a vision of something so amazing that you have been left in awe but at the next moment questioning God saying "I see what you are showing me but how am I going to get there?" The scope of the vision can be so much grander than our understanding that we quit on it before we even begin the journey to get there. The key is that God doesn't require our understanding. The vision is given to us for His glory, and that vision can only be attained by His power at work in us. Daughter of God, if the Lord has given you a vision of marriage, if He has already revealed your husband to you, if He just has you making a list of the qualities you are

looking for in a God ordained spouse, we are all on different levels on this journey. Maybe you just desire marriage but have not yet gone to your Heavenly Father about it, know that He is more than able. If you have made a list, you may end up rewriting it a couple of times over this journey as the Lord grows, matures, empowers and heals you. Trust the Lord's ability. He is the omnipotent one and His power is in you, therefore every vision, dream, destiny and purpose set before you will be accomplished for His glory.

"For God has not given us a spirit of fear, but of power and of love and of a sound mind."
~ 2 Timothy1:7

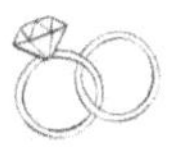

One of the greatest battles we face in seasons of waiting is FEAR. Fear has the ability to not only cripple us, but also keep us in bondage if we allow it to take root. When we give fear a door with which to operate, we can quickly find ourselves spiraling down a rabbit hole. Fear can start with a feeling, something similar to an anxiousness that you do not understand. It can also start with giving a runaway thought a voice or even having an internal dialogue with it. One of the challenges I've had to face in my life time again and again is that internal dialogue of conversation with a fearful thought that often in the past led me to an emotional breakdown. Thank God that He is a patient and kind, healing God. See the enemy of our soul sends fearful darts into our mind with the intention of stealing our soundness of mind and corrupting the truth of our identity and the word of God hidden in our hearts. Strategies he may have but victory he does not. Satan uses the stronghold of fear as a type of bondage to keep us powerless. We cannot operate in the power of God from a place of fear, because fear takes the place of authority and the place of faith and belief-the cornerstones of our walk with God. Without faith and belief we are powerless. It is a vicious cycle we can get caught up in. When fear comes in like a thief during this journey to marriage, set a counter attack against it declaring the word against the enemy. With a shout declaring "You Lord have not giving me a spirit of fear but of power and of love and of a sound mind." The word of God says that if we resist the devil he will flee. Resist the stronghold of fear. The Holy Spirit gives you the strength to endure singleness, to resist all pressure to quit, to focus on your purpose not just your relationship status. Meditating on this scripture encourages us to have boldness over all anxiety. The power of the Holy

Spirit helps us to manage our desires; to love and value God's timing; helps us to exercise self control; to set healthy boundaries; to prevent the panic we feel when we focus on our singleness; helps us to build a confident God centered life until the destined partner arrives. If we choose to love God's plan and timing more than the desire for quick companionship we will trust His provision. We should use wisdom to set boundaries, resist temptation, and make wise choices, avoiding rushed decisions driven by lust and anxiety, this will protect our future marriages. Remember that your identity is not in being married but in Christ. Knowing our identity allows us to wait with all confidence, not in desperation, and it allows us to build a life of purpose now.

"For the Lord God is a sun and shield;
The Lord will give grace and glory;
No good thing will He withhold
From those who walk uprightly."
~Psalm 84:11

We have the assurance, as His single daughters, that God is our protector (shield) and provider (sun), and will not deny us a truly good marriage if we live righteously. The wait is for His perfect timing, developing character and ensuring the right fit, turning the waiting season into a season of growth and preparation for that blessing, not a sign of denial. Remember when you were a toddler and there used to be these toys that you had to fit the shape into its proper notch and it would fall into the cube or basket. Well that's us. God is working on you and your spouse separately until your ready to come together as the right fit. God is our source of good and marriage is a good gift. God's promise to us is NOT to withhold good things. If you're waiting it's because He's preparing you and the blessing for it's best form. Teaching us reliance first. We must live a life of integrity, purity (in thought and action) and obedience to God. Think about David in the Bible. He was anointed as king, but had to wait for his appointed time to take his rightful place. In the wait for that appointed time he prepared, fighting battles in the very field he was anointed in. Delay is not denial. That's the problem. Whenever God tells us "no" we get upset thinking its a forever kind of no- sometimes that's the case- and sometimes its a not yet because He is working behind the scenes preparing us-His daughters and His sons-making our eventual blessing more profound. David fought lions before he fought Goliath. God is our shield and sun; He protects us from wrong choices and gives grace. In Him we find fulfillment and protection. Your worth is NOT dependent on finding a spouse, it is found in God.

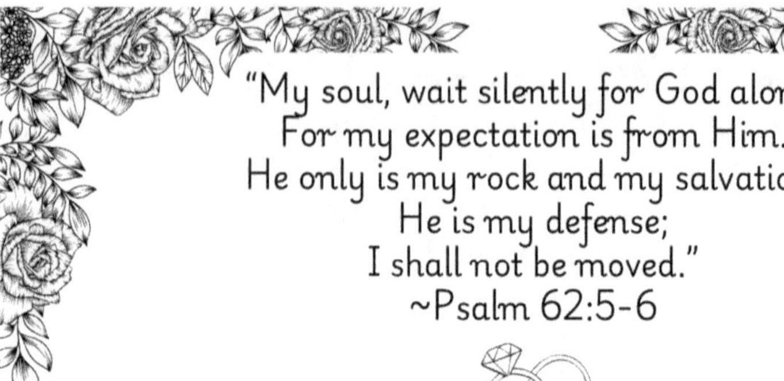

Could you imagine what it would be like if we became the Davids' of our season? He is commanding his "soul to wait silently for God alone". David was a man-often flawed- that the word of God says was a man after God's own heart. Not only did David know how to repent, but knew something just as important. His sole reliance was on God. He acknowledged that his "Expectation is from Him". He acknowledged that he put all of himself, his entire hope; trust; reliance; safety; deliverance and future in God. Temptation still came, but he willingly and intentionally would turn his attention back to God. David calls God his ONLY rock and salvation. The Hebrews word for rock is Tsuwr meaning cliff, boulder, refuge. He called God his defense; proclaiming that he would not be moved. Ask yourself today, am I facing my waiting season the way David faced his life and his walk with God? Is my sole reliance on God and because of that I am putting all of myself in the palm of His hand, not just pieces but my entire self? When temptation comes am I willingly and intentionally turning my attention back to God or am I flirting with temptation and danger? Are you allowing God to be your refuge and your defense or are you allowing the stresses and frustrations of the waiting, cause you to run away from His protection? Are you proclaiming to the Heavens and the Earth in an unshakable way that you shall not be moved? This is an opportunity to draw closer to God as David did. You will find no other place of refuge, fulfillment, reliance protection than the God of your salvation.

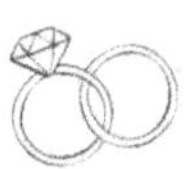

God is the author of your love story. Not just the marital love at the end of this waiting season, but if you look over your life I'm sure moments will jump out at you like a carousel of snapshots of love that you know only God could have done it in that specific way for that specific memory. When you look back over your life, are there moments that vividly stand out to you, that God was showing you how much He loves you. I know that sometimes embarrassing memories or low moments in our past seem to stand out creating a noisy space in our mind, distracting us from God's love for us in action. Instead focusing our attention on developing the characteristics of love, patience and endurance while trusting God's plan and timing should be our priority. We can't just "put on" love, patience and endurance. We have to actually live it, the way Jesus lived it, as an extension of Himself. We as individuals stump our growth when we choose our own moral standards as a measure for love patience and endurance when we should be developing said virtues by demonstrating them in all the actions we take and in the way we communicate and collaborate with others. Using this period of waiting as a surrender to God, allowing him to develop our character can be tough. The trials that come and expose, and reveal the weaknesses in our character are hard to face but face them we must. Why must we face them? So that only the faith, love, and hope of God remains. Not our standard but His. It is a continual laying down of ourselves and a resurrection in Him. The nature of love is endurance. Look at what Jesus endured on the cross for all humanity. The greatest act of love of all time. Could you endure something similar in the name of love? Lets admit just for a moment that there are times love ain't easy-especially with family. Now onto hope. Hope does not mean passively waiting. I'll be truthful. I started this journey believing that just because I was God's daughter, that the husband He promised He was just going to bring that man to my door. Very naive and entitled thinking, but I quickly learned that hope truly means continually actively growing and being prepared for the future while trusting God's perfect timing. You've heard me say to give yourself grace. Now I will also tell you to be patient with yourself as you journey through the waiting. Also be patient with others-some just won't be able to comprehend where God has you. Not every Christian believes that God chooses your spouse, they may tell you that God wants you to choose or that you are waiting in vain for something that God wants you to decide. In my case I wait because I asked God to choose for me and, so I trust that He will and I endure aiming to cultivate the characteristics of love, faith, and hope daily until it's not something I emulate but who I've become.

"Indeed, let no one who waits on You be ashamed;
Let those be ashamed who deal treacherously without cause."
~Psalm 25:3

I truly have come to the realization that waiting on God in silence is a challenge of faith, but at the same time a source of peace. Not the type of silence that you will not speak to God about your needs or desires, but the silence that speaks only between you and God and no one else. When you are strolling or battling through a season of waiting on a promise and you don't hold your silence around others doubts start to creep in. Often times if the person you are sharing with is not on the same level as you-you can start to feel ashamed about waiting on something that seemed possible at first but now has become impossible in your eyes. The ones around you may not be saying things to hurt you but the enemy uses them to sow those seeds. What happens when we get ashamed of our waiting? What happens when we get ashamed of voicing our desire for the promises we believe God has given us to Him who put them there in the first place? This stops us from praying those promises through because we become embarrassed to continue to go to God about it and abandon the promise which eventually leads us to walking away. The word makes the declaration "Let no one who waits on you be ashamed" why? Because the one you are waiting on is faithful to complete what He says. Because no one whose not in the room when your promises are given to you by God-can understand the profound need within you for them to be fulfilled, or the certainty within you when your spirit bears witness with the words the Lord speaks to you and over you. For a little background. In October 2012 I received a promise from Lord that in a year I would conceive a son and I was to call him Jeremiah. Well I remember getting so excited because I

had never received a word like that before. For the next year I began to get more frustrated each month because it didn't happen. My family by this point was thinking I was crazy except for my mother-in-law and my father-in-law at the time. I started to feel embarrassed and ashamed, but of course God came through like always. October 2013 I found out I was pregnant. I knew it was a boy because the Lord had said so, but because I had not kept quiet in the wait, for the following months I was the target for the jokes implying that the "son" I thought God had said the baby would be-was in fact going to be a girl. When I started to buy baby clothes for boys the jokes got worse but in the end Jeremiah was born, and God got the glory in that and all the things that came after but that is a story for another day. I did eventually have a girl four years later. When we don't keep things silent we open the door to this flood of negativity that often shames us instead of learning the talent of the "shh" or the "shush." God does not reveal things to us and then bring us through seasons of waiting and preparation to shame us, it is to give us hope and build our faith and He does NOT go back on what He says. That is our assurance.

"For since the beginning of the world
Men have not heard nor perceived by the ear,
Nor has the eye seen any God besides You,
Who acts for the one who waits for Him."
~Isaiah 64:4

Faith activates grace. Waiting either builds your faith and strengthens it-as long as you keep your eyes on God- or it breaks you. If you take your eyes off of "the one who acts for the one who waits for Him" and instead put your focus on the delays; the rejections; the insecurity and frustrations that come when you try to find your life partner and spouse on your own you will find no one up to your standard. Ouch! I know that sounds rough but it is true for some of us. Let me be transparent here. Once I told God I wanted to join a bible study for singles. Not for dating but to meet new people, and maybe form connections because I was feeling somewhat lonely. Well I got a firm immediate "No" from Holy Spirit. Then I heard Him say "Your husband isn't there," which I already knew, but that desire for connection was strong in me. So of course I tried to make excuses to God. "I wasn't going to go looking for someone to date, just potential friends. At this point came the revelation. My motivation may not have been to look for a spouse at this bible study but the others were there for the purpose connecting with someone to spend their life with. Now I'm going to take it up a notch and say something not everyone may agree with. There is absolutely nothing wrong with singles bible studies, or marrying a good christian husband, but here is the shoe drop. If you are called to ministry, and I don't mean just in your home or out in the streets, more of like missionary work; pastoring; evangelizing; if ministry is your life's work and you know the burden, weight and oil that you carry- allow God to choose for you. I say this because you will need a spouse that helps you carry your oil and burden without any insecurity getting in the way. You

will also want a spouse who also carries oil and understands the weight of it. Being unequally yolked doesn't just apply to a believer and unbeliever married to each other. You can be married to someone who does not desire to go as high or as intimate with God as you, causing you to be unequally yolked, which brings strain to the relationship. Wait on the God "who acts for him or her in this case, who waits for Him." He is the God that has always been. The one and only true God to ever be seen or heard, you better believe His hand is all over you and your future marriage.

Did you know that there is such a thing as bad courage I didn't, so I never gave it any thought until I sat with God and did my research before the devotional for this day. The difference between good courage and bad courage according to google is that good courage comes from a place of possibility, a heart of faith or a focus on compassion and empathy, all things that are the root and fruit of our relationship with Christ and living our life submitted to God and walking according to the Holy Spirit. This verse gives us the assurance that if we operate from a place of good courage and hope together he will strengthen us. During this waiting have you been of good courage or have you been of bad courage trying to force things to happen of your own will instead of God's will? Bad courage according to google is that it is often set in motion by reactionary emotions, fear, pride, or the lust of the flesh. This waiting journey definitely has its ups and its downs. I've felt fear that I've heard the Lord incorrectly. Have you? I've had ugly moments of pride, where I've said reactionary things to God I'm not proud of. Have you? I've questioned this desire for marriage and the husband God is preparing for me has been God breathed or lust of the flesh bred. Have you? It is part of the process.

"But may the God of all grace, who called us to His eternal glory by Christ Jesus, after you have suffered a while, perfect, establish, strengthen, and settle you."
~1 Peter 5:10

Waiting. Waiting is a test. It's not a pass or fail test. It is a quality test before a product can be declared finished. Think of a block of clay (that's us)on a potter's wheel. The block of clay is spinning on the wheel with water (the Holy Spirit), and shaped and molded by the master's (God's) hand. Before it goes in the oven its got to be looked over for imperfections, anything that may have come to the surface during the molding process that will have to be removed because it will mar and alter the piece from it's intended design. Then it's baked. The paint and the glaze are placed on it (Jesus and His blood) and then it's completed. Our waiting season is a quality test meant to expose to us areas that still need surrendered, expose hidden hurt, hidden bitterness, hidden unforgiveness, deep things that at times we are unaware are there. At the same time waiting is a preparation. Those exposed things are given time to be weeded out and healed and the new transformed you can emerge in preparation to receive the promise of marriage. Trust and believe that your God ordained spouse is going through the same. Remember its not only about you its about them too. You want to be able to come together as two halves who are healed, to make one whole in Christ. Testing and preparation can feel like suffering if we take our understanding away from the true purpose behind it. God doesn't cause us to wait because He wants us to suffer. God's testing and preparation perfects His work and will in us, it establishes His purpose in and for our lives, it strengthens us in our walk with Him, and it settles us. Know that the testing and preparation, the waiting won't last forever. Instead of running from it, lean into it. Understanding that it is for your benefit and that of your soon to come groom.

"Let us hold fast the confession of our hope without wavering, for He who promised is faithful."
~Hebrews 10:23

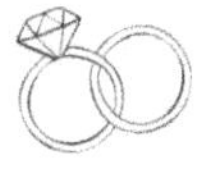

When the subject of being unwavering comes up in a conversation of faith, Christian living etcetera, sometimes we may feel inadequate in that area. I know I have because there have been seasons where I myself have been like a reed wavering in the wind, and I have been shakable where I have needed to be unshakable. We cannot be unwavering in our own strength, especially when it really matters. Have you ever been a keyboard warrior? Where you have been on social media and you've seen a post you don't agree with and an unwavering spirit hits your spine and you just have to argue your point of view? That's a fleshly unwavering Spirit and we cannot operate from that place or position because it is only temporary. God's faithfulness is something we can see over and over again in scripture, we see His faithfulness in our lives, in the lives of our brothers and sisters in Christ. His faithfulness does not and cannot fail. When we confess our hope in God, we are declaring a hope that He Himself has placed in us, and if we focus on that truth it will assist us in being unwavering. Be sure that what you are confessing is God placed hope and not flesh led desire. Self examine and drive out all fleshly hope, desire and repent allowing God's will to take it's place.

"He did not waver at the promise of God through unbelief, but was strengthened in faith, giving glory to God, and being fully convinced that what He had promised He was also able to perform."
~ Romans 4:20-21

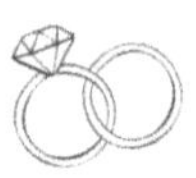

Are you fully convinced that what God has promised you, He is able to perform? This journey of waiting is definitely not for the weak at heart, although there will be times that you will be stripped and pruned to the point of weakness. Even then the Lord will provide you His strength. The road to the promises of God are rarely smooth. There are tests along the way, as well as pitfalls from the enemy-mostly attacks on your mind-but we must raise a standard against unbelief. It must be an unwavering standard. When we determine within our spirit and mind to tare down every lie of the enemy that contradicts the word and promises of God-that's when the attack of unbelief comes. You must raise the standard and declare your strength in the Lord, declare your faith and give glory to God and push the enemy back. If you resist his attack he has no choice but to flee. If you are struggling declare with power and authority "I am fully convinced that what God has promised He is able to perform" say it until you believe it, declare it until it becomes real to you.

There are allot of themes across the word of God, especially about salvation, trust, about His strength and not being afraid. See the Lord created us and knew the struggles we would face, but He also gave us the answer to overcome. When it comes to relationships it can be easy to blur the lines and go from depending on God's salvation to the person you are in relationship with. Not just marital relationships but friendships, and familial relationships as well. We can easily go from going to God for answers, and comfort-to venting to those friends and family members, which then leads to a circle of voices in our thoughts that can give opposing counsel to what God is calling you to do, and then all these other voices become voices of salvation overriding God. This Journey of preparing for marriage, waiting on the marriage promise can be extremely hard. One thing I've learned is that silence may be required. Even when tempted, keeping silence to the people I'm in a relationship with. Why? Because the circle of voices opining gets louder than God's voice and it has led me to confusion and doubt, so now I trust God and God alone. On this journey if you need a physical person for accountability in this season, and for clarity, ask God who. The trust in our covenant relationship with God is a result of a history where He has come through again and again. It is also a sign of our obedience. We obey He trusts us with more. Every direction He leads you on this journey, obey. Every unction He leads you to do as part of a prophetic act, obey even if it doesn't make sense, you just might be having a Noah experience marriage journey, Just as an example I will share the following story. The Lord had me

make a Mattah (Rod) for the husband He told me is coming.
I'm crafty but never had I worked with wood before or done
something as complex but I obeyed and He showed me what
to do and sent me someone to help. The Mattah was
beautiful upon completion. The gift turned out to be
something needed as he was learning to take back territory
in the Spirit. He is our song so celebrate. Celebrate all the
things you know are coming because He is in it. Even
celebrate the delays because that will make the fulfillment
that much sweeter.

Strength In The Waiting

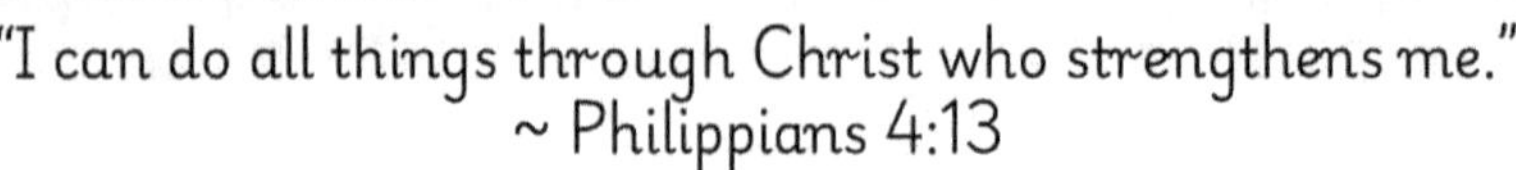

"I can do all things through Christ who strengthens me."
~ Philippians 4:13

Christ is the door by which we are able to do all things which we could not do in and of our own strength. There have been many times where I've had to literally say to the Lord, "I can't do this. Love this person, forgive that person unless you give me your heart in this situation," and every time He comes through. When the marriage promise finally arrives there will be many times when this scripture will come back to mind and be an anchor for you. It doesn't say it is possible to do all things, it says "I can do all things." Christ Himself reminding us that He has no doubt in our abilities and capabilities as long as we do it through the door that He is. We must remember that once married the work really begins. There will be times our flesh will want to give in and give up, walking away because it will have deceived us into believing that things are just too hard. Let me say to you that I've been there and I kept pushing and trying but in my own strength and I couldn't fix the problem. I kept at it until the Lord showed me that in the situation that I was in, it was a futile effort. That time and that "mess" were all of my doing. I disobeyed and went my own way instead of heeding the Lord's warnings. I learned the hard Lesson and it's why I will take every advantage to be had out of this journey, so that when the promise is fulfilled and the real work begins I can truly walk out the "I can do all things through Christ." Nothing worth having and keeping ever comes easy. Here are some declarations that you can speak to increase your faith, strength and hope:
"I can forgive because God forgives."
"I can love despite being hurt because God loves despite being rejected."
"I can love despite feeling angry."

"I can be kind even to someone proving to be an assignment from the enemy."
"I can love my spouse even when he does not live up to my expectation."
"I can yield my desire to be right and win an argument with my husband, if the occasion ever arises."
"I can be respectful even when I feel disrespected."
"I can submit to my husband even when I am afraid it can be interpreted as the right for them to control me."
"I can, I can, I can do all things-even those things that feel hard; impossible, frustrating, and unfair. All of these things I can do through Christ because I am not doing it in my own strength. No I am entering through the door of His strength which gives me the ability to accomplish the hard, the impossible, the frustrating and the unfair."

This psalm can be applied to seasons of waiting by reminding us to stay focused on the main source of our strength and protection, God, instead of leaning on our own efforts or anxiousness about finding a partner. Lets be real, anxiety has the power to cripple an individual, leaning on those feelings would not be a great source to help finding a partner, you would attract the wrong kind of person. This scripture reminds us that we do not have to go on this journey of waiting trying to figure out the directions and the terrain in our own limited strength, which will only lead to exhaustion and anxiety. What we should be doing instead is drawing from the well of God's divine strength to build our life, and pursue the things we are passionate about. If marriage and a partner are the only things that you are passionate about then you will find yourself unfulfilled. God is our shield. He is our defender and protector at all times especially during the vulnerable moments of the waiting season. Trusting that He Himself is our shield helps us to resist temptation to "settle" for an ungodly or incompatible partner out of impatience or the very really fear of being alone. He protects us from potential pain and regret. Regret is not only a feeling but a horrible place to find yourself in, not many are able to fight their way back from it. The most profound way to apply this verse to your journey is to actively trust. Its a give and take. We place our confidence in His perfect timing and plan, and then we are assured of His help. Don't try to make a relationship work on your own timeline. We must live surrendered. Surrendering our worries and believing He desires what is best for us continually.

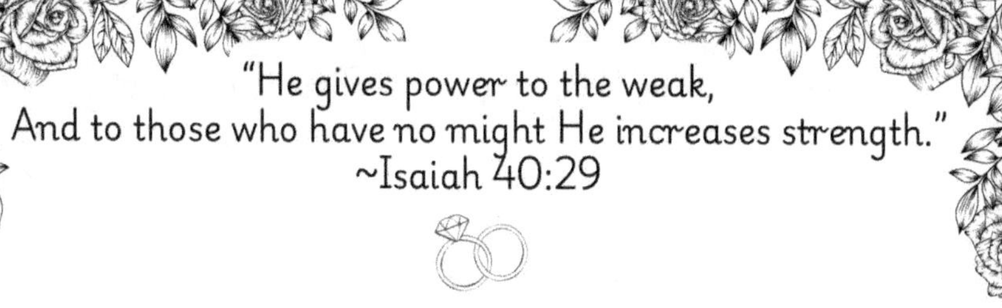

Lord thank you that when I feel weak you step in with your power and empower me. Lord thank you that in the moments that I feel myself withering in the strength to keep pushing, believing and pressing on, that you increase my strength. You are my source and as long as I keep my eyes on YOU-and not on what I see or don't see happening in the natural-I will always be comforted because I know that you neither slumber nor sleep, which means that your hand is on it all. Lord strengthen my capacity and ability to trust you. Lord strengthen me in the area of doubt and disbelief and to take you at your word because "you are not a man that you should lie nor the son of man that you should repent. Have you not said and shall you not make it good." Father in heaven there are moments I have no might to my name, or to this waiting challenge that often feels like a fight against myself, but then your presence; grace and strength enter the moment and cover me. I am so thankful I have you in Jesus name. Amen.

"And He said to me, "My grace is sufficient for you, for My strength is made perfect in weakness." Therefore most gladly I will rather boast in my infirmities, that the power of Christ may rest upon me."
~2 Corinthians 12:9

In moments of trials and struggles we as believers fall back on "my grace is sufficient" and because this flesh is always focused on discontent and seeking only what it pleases- if we are not submitted in the spirit then we can find ourselves believing that His grace is not sufficient and that will take the place of actual truth. Be so saturated in truth that the lie in fact never becomes our distorted reality. Have you ever questioned if God's strength REQUIRES our weakness in order to be perfect? If we are always trying to be strong or put up a front of strength to others, then where are we giving God room to move and work or give us his strength? Our fleshly strength is flawed and in no way compares to His own supernatural strength. The world teaches us that weakness is something to be ashamed of while covenant relationship with Christ teaches us that our weakness is the door by which He can work, it teaches us submission and humility. Paul wrote that he would "most gladly rather boast in his infirmities, that the power of Christ would rest upon him," So I challenge you. If you feel weak cry out to God about your weaknesses, during this waiting room experience, not in complaint but to make it clear to Him and to remind yourself that Christ's power is the source of our strength and our ability to carry-on even when we feel we are beyond capacity of what we can handle. His grace that leads to His strength in our weakness is all that we need to make it on this journey. When the road gets a little bumpy and tough Hold on to this.

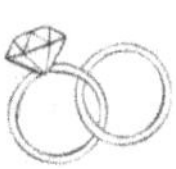

Have you ever been in a season where the Lord has placed a song in your heart that ministers to you and gets you through, gives you the strength to keep pushing towards breakthrough. I've been through seasons where the only thing I had to hold on to, was the song He placed in the wells of my heart and spirit. In this season of waiting the song that has sustained me has been "Blessed assurance." There are some lyrics in that song that just grip me in profound ways. "He's been the fourth man in the fire." Let's be real for a moment. Waiting definitely feels like being in the fiery furnace of insecurity, doubt, indecision, weariness, the desire to quit-give up and give in, giving the term "trial by fire" a whole new meaning. Then there's another line, "what He did for me on Calvary is more than enough." We need to understand and know that what He has ALREADY DONE should be enough and anything else is just the icing and the decorations on the cake, and because He is our Savior Redeemer He desires to give us good things. The lyrics go on to say, "Perfect submission, all is at rest I know the author of tomorrow has ordered my steps." This brought me to a place where I had to question myself about what my submission to God looked like, was it the posture of a heart at rest? Knowing that He has not only ordered our steps but that He has also written our love story. Don't just know with your mind but know that you know in your inner most being. Then comes the clincher of lyrics, "I will trust in God my Savior, the one who will never fail." The Lord wasn't just our Savior at the cross. He is still the Savior in whom we can trust completely and will never fail to this day. Surrender

of ourselves needs to happen in order for trust to take place. He saves us from the snares of the enemy, He saves us from ourselves, He saves us even when we don't heed his warnings. He is our salvation. What song has given you the Lord's strength in this waiting season? What song is ministering to you and reigniting your hope that He will fulfill every promise He's ever made you? Not even one promise will slip from His thoughts or His hands. Sing that song and allow it to breathe life into you again. Sing that song until it becomes a cry to God. Sing it until you see the full manifestation of what He has promised you.

"Be strong and of good courage, do not fear nor be afraid of them; for the Lord your God, He is the One who goes with you. He will not leave you nor forsake you."
~ Deuteronomy 31:6

Being strong during waiting seasons, reminds me of a roller coaster ride at times. A slow steady ascent of faith, a pause at the peak and then a sharp rapid decent with sharp turns that knock us around in weariness; in doubt and even fear and then it cycles again. In this scripture verse it calls us to not only be strong but also to be of good courage. Courage here is the Hebrew word "amats" which means "to be alert." On a roller coaster ride if you keep your eyes open you can anticipate the curves, the ascents and the descents and avoid being caught by surprise or knocked around. On the other hand, if you're like me and ride the beast with your eyes closed, you have no choice but to go with the flow and just pray you aren't bruised by the end of the ride. I want my season of waiting to be more than just a go with the flow and just survive by the seat of my pants situation. I want to learn to be strong in the Lord and to be alert not only for every leading of the Holy Spirit but every snare of the enemy. Don't be deceived in believing that the enemy of our soul, satan, and his minions aren't actively trying to draw us away from our promises; attempting to get us to throw in the towel and give up; throwing arrows of distraction and doubt; having us occupied with minor scuffles and battles so that when we are finally at the point of breakthrough we are so battle weary there's no more fight left in us. The Lord Himself calls us to not be afraid.

"It is God who arms me with strength,
And makes my way perfect."
~Psalm 18:32

What does it feel like when you attempt to do things in your own strength? For me I feel awkward, like I'm fumbling around trying to carry a shield and a sword too big for me. The way I imagine David felt at first when he went to face Goliath, and they tried to arm him in ill-fitting armor. What did David do? David stripped himself of all of that and he stepped into the strength with which God armed him with. He stepped up with sling shot in hand knowing that the strength and power of God were with him. In this waiting season you need to not only know but understand that this season is a powerful one. It's powerful because if you use the time wisely- you are growing, bonding and developing a deeper covenant relationship with your creator who is also your Father in Heaven. It's powerful because He is equipping you, training you, and surrounding you with His presence care and provision. Take your eyes from everything and everyone except Him. In this waiting God is arming you in His strength and making your way perfect. The path to your promise, and your God ordained husband will be full of obstacles and pitfalls, but the Lord Himself will arm you with strength, and if you walk step in step with Him in obedience and discernment the way will be perfect. Perfect even with delays, rejections, lack of communication, through trials, arguments and misunderstandings, no matter what your eyes see how your heart feels but by what your spirit knows and understands and by the strength of God that He has armed you with.

God's Sovereignty & Guidance

Dearest Father in Heaven, incline your ear to us today and hear the prayer of our hearts. Help us to get out of our own way, to give up any plans that we have created in our hearts. Help us Jesus to surrender our hearts and therefore our plans to you and turn our focus on allowing you to direct our paths. Father, hear the cry of my heart that says "It's hard and I don't know if I can do what you are asking of me." Father in Heaven help me to hold on to the assurance that every plan you have for me is bigger and better than any plan I could have fostered in my heart for any part of my life. Holy Spirit help me to discern the difference between the steps that have been ordered for me and the plans I've made on my own so that I live my life always according to the will of God and never the will of my flesh. Loneliness is hard. Singleness is hard. Waiting is hard. If we just put our eyes on you, you will make the burden lighter. Lord, we love you and honor you and we are thankful you take such care in ordering our steps. Help us to remain peaceful in your plan even when we don't have all the facts before us. Let us remember that you are good and therefore your plan is good, nothing in your plan will ever hurts us, only bring us closer to you. Lord seal us until the day that your promise comes to fruition and then seal us and our husbands to be, until the day of redemption. In Jesus name, the name above every other name we pray. Amen.

"The Lord will guide you continually,
And satisfy your soul in drought,
And strengthen your bones;
You shall be like a watered garden,
And like a spring of water, whose waters do not fail."
~Isaiah 58:11

If you are one that is on this marriage journey, and God Himself has told you who your husband is, but you are in a season where there is no communication, and so you feel as if your soul is in a drought, Jehovah Jireh Himself will satisfy you if you just hang on to Him. If you are one that is going through a season of loneliness as well as waiting, and feel as if your soul is in drought Jehovah Himself will satisfy your soul if you wrap yourself in His presence. Elohim Himself created you with a built-in wellspring on the inside. This verse promises that "you shall be like a watered garden, and like a spring of water, whose waters do not fail". According to John 7:38 "He that believes on me, as the scripture hath said, out of his belly shall flow rivers of living water". This means that if you stir up the waters from the wellspring that He created in you when He formed you in your mother's womb, then in every season of drought His living water will flow up inside of you and water your soul. His living water in you will never fail. Psalm 23:2-3 says "He makes me to lie down in green pastures; He leads me beside the still waters. He restores my soul; He leads me in the paths of righteousness For His name's sake." The Lord leads. He not only leads you, but He leads you to places of restoration and sustenance. It is His intrinsic nature. We need to understand that EVERYTHING including our future marriages are for His namesake and bringing glory to His name and kingdom.

"I will instruct you and teach you in the way you should go;
I will guide you with My eye."
~Psalm 32:8

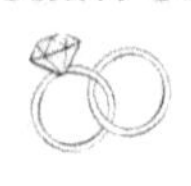

In His written word Jesus has been referred to as "Rabboni" which translates from the Aramaic to "Lord teacher-master" which is a sign of deep respect but also a sign of a personal relationship between the speaker and Jesus. See John 20:16 and John 13:14. In the waiting, it is a time of deepening the personal relationship between you and Jesus. Let Him teach and instruct you in all His ways so that when the appointed time comes you are more than ready. As I write this devotional I see clearly in a vision a needle. Sewing needles come with eyes in all sizes, but in our personal walk with Jesus there is truly only one size fits all not all sizes fit us individually. His eye is the standard by which we should always be led. His eye can see what we cannot. His perspective grander and all encompassing. If we take the opportunity to deepen our relationship with Him, we become the thread that easily passes through said eye without multiple attempts to get it right. The deeper our personal relationship the more freely we will be able to follow His instructions and teaching in all the ways we should go. Think of what a beautiful resource it is when the intimacy of relationship with Jesus helps us and gives us powerful insight into our future marital relationship.

The line between the plans in our hearts and the Lord's counsel can be thin sometimes. Discernment is necessary. We should ask ourselves what is more important to us. Is it the plans we've made in our hearts-that then transition into visions and desires-or the Lord's counsel. In waiting seasons, it is our biggest opportunity to let go of all our plans and expectations and give them to God. The more that we let go and give things over to Him, the easier it will get to submit to the Lord's counsel. For the Lord's counsel to stand we must live a life of surrender. Surrendering to God is not a one time thing, it is a lifestyle. For some of us it'll be daily, for some seasonally, for some situationally. Surrender brings transformation. Marriage takes teamwork. In a Marriage the wife fulfills the man, and the husband fulfills the woman. We each have what the other needs, but how we direct what the other needs can only be done with the Lord's counsel. Our own plans let us down on occasion, but the Lord's counsel is a constant life changing thing. It transforms us, it lifts us up, it leads us. Following His counsel can only ever lead to Him bringing us to new heights and new revelations. It is written in Proverbs 3:5 to not lean unto our own understanding but in all our ways to acknowledge Him. We make plans based on our own understanding and logic, often forgetting to include Him, especially if we know it is something that He would not approve of. We acknowledge Him by allowing His counsel to stand and take precedent in our lives. While you wait, still yourself and let His counsel be the standard by which you are led. Let His counsel be the measure by which you are found to surpass in all things.

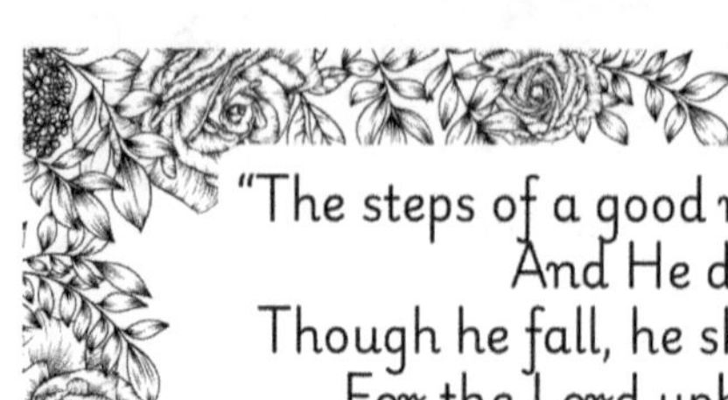

What makes you a good woman? Have you ever thought about what characteristics of your personality make you a good woman? How does God order your steps in those specific areas of your character? Let's look at this from God's perspective. Elohim not only created you, but He created every characteristic of your personality, and He delights in you. Even when you stumble and you fall, He picks you up again. In this season of waiting have you had moments when you railed at God and said some of the following "Daddy I'm tired of waiting", "God I don't want to do this anymore", "God I need more patience without the trials to get there". I may have said some of these a time or two. Thank God He is so gracious and merciful, He does not let us stay where we fall but rather picks us back up. Let's choose this day to have God's perspective, the same characteristics of His grace and His mercy going forward in our marriages. There will be times when our husbands will fall and stumble, or we will fall and stumble, and the challenge will be in our response. Will we leave one another where we stumbled and cast one another down or will we choose to uphold one another with the grace and mercy of God? Will we then grow together to be good women and men of God so that He delights in our way as a kingdom couple who glorifies Him and walks in His way? Uphold each other and watch God uphold your marriage.

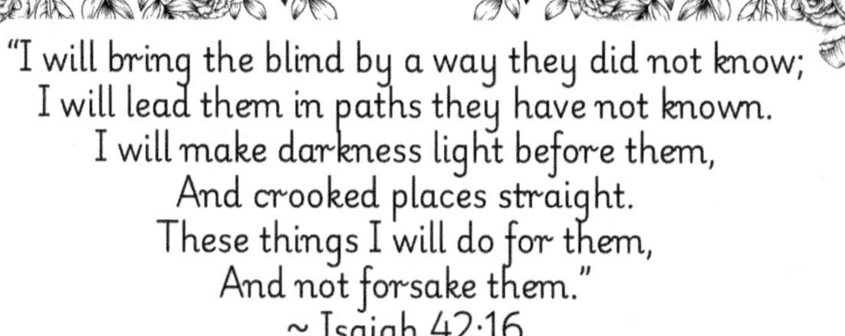

"I will bring the blind by a way they did not know;
I will lead them in paths they have not known.
I will make darkness light before them,
And crooked places straight.
These things I will do for them,
And not forsake them."
~ Isaiah 42:16

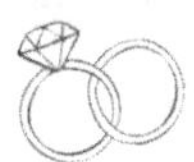

There are times in the waiting seasons of life that you can begin to feel blind. I have told God in moments of weariness, "God I feel like I'm walking blind." Every time His response is, "trust me." You may be feeling blind because what God has spoken to you in your times of intimacy in the secret place, has not been confirmed to you by another brother or sister in Christ and you only have what He has spoken to you to go on. Moments like these can cause us to feel like darkness is setting in, especially in the sense that we begin to doubt that we heard God say what He said. We doubt our own discernment of His voice which is a tactic of the enemy, with no light to be found. Some paths that God calls us to walk in, during seasons of waiting, are unknown to us but not unknown to Him. Remember, He goes before us. Psalm 119:105 says that His word is a lamp unto our feet and a light to our path. Our Heavenly Father loves us so much that He will not allow us to stay in darkness but illuminates the way to lead us out. When our waiting seasons take crooked paths away from the victory waiting for us at the end of the journey, He still sweeps in and turns the crooked turns straight and brings us back to where we need to be. God does not forsake you in the waiting. There are times where we want Him to give us all the answers from the beginning, so that we don't have to walk blind, and we can pass every test; every challenge; overcome every obstacle with flying colors but what would be the actual benefit of that? There would be none, because we would not grow at all. We wouldn't need Him at all if He told us everything. We need to position our thoughts to receive what information He reveals to us when He reveals it to us. Even when we feel it comes to us at a trickle He controls the flow nonetheless.

"Behold, I send an Angel before you to keep you in the way and to bring you into the place which I have prepared."
~Exodus 23:20

When reading scripture have you come across the phrase "The Angel of the Lord"? That is often noted as a reference to Jesus. Jesus is leading the way on this journey and it is our responsibility and privilege to follow step by step behind Him so that our steps do not falter because He indeed will lead us to the place or person He Himself has prepared for us. Jesus is leading us in order to guard and direct us. He is our sovereign Lord therefore His plan is sovereign. His sovereignty guarantees that we reach the destiny He has purposed. The hardest part of this journey other than the wait, is believing and trusting that He is working even when it's not visible to our eyesight. As hard as it might be, our duty during this period is to stay in communion with God; to trust and obey; so that every direction during this period is clear to us and that it brings us closer to His purpose for our life and future marriages. During this waiting season one of our greatest works is to address our sinful predilections. Our spirit must overcome our flesh so that we may develop a godly character. When we sit at at His feet we are able to learn valuable lessons and grow through true companionship as He prepares our heart to be godly spouses. Jesus, as the Angel of the Lord carries God's name and has authority. Only through a deep obedient relationship with Jesus, not faking it till we make it by following rules, will we enter that prepared place called marriage.

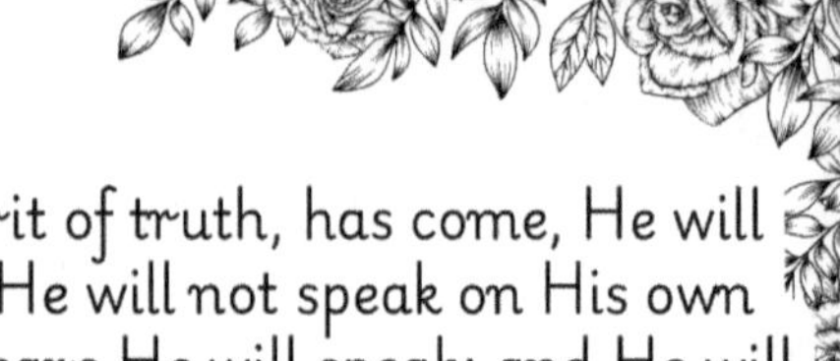

"However, when He, the Spirit of truth, has come, He will guide you into all truth; for He will not speak on His own authority, but whatever He hears He will speak; and He will tell you things to come."
~John 16:13

Holy Spirit is the Spirit of Truth. Let that sink in for a minute. He does not, will not, and cannot lie. That in itself is powerful. He will guide you. The reason that we make mistakes is because we attempt to do things in our own will, following what we believe to be true. We believe in our own misguided logic, rather than the written; irrefutable; and unmistakable truth of God. It is written that the Holy Spirit does not speak on His own authority, that whatever He hears He speaks. That means that if you are in tune with Him, He will not lead you in the wrong way. It is written that He will tell you things to come. In this waiting season Holy Spirit will reveal to you all the information you need to pray for your incoming marriage. He will speak prayer points to you about your future husband. At the beginning of my journey, I prayed a specific prayer. I asked the Lord to choose my husband for me-because I did not trust myself to choose for myself having made mistakes before. I was putting my trust in the Lord. When you put your trust in the Lord, all things will turn out as they were meant to.

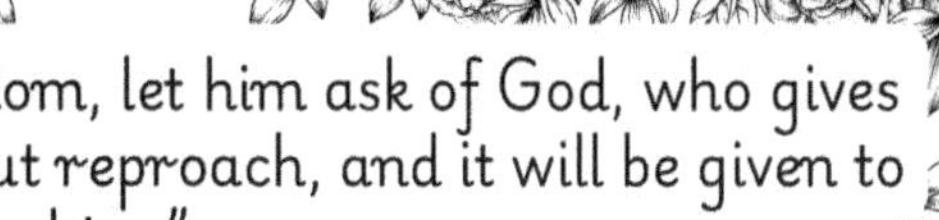

"If any of you lacks wisdom, let him ask of God, who gives to all liberally and without reproach, and it will be given to him."
~James 1:5

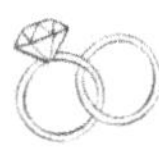

Being a wife will require a supernatural wisdom that only God can provide. There is no one who will know your husband and his needs better than the Lord. Most importantly the Lord knows his heart, raw and the healed places that still remain in him. The supernatural wisdom of God will allow you to become the helpmate He designed you to be and the layered one your husband needs. Don't ever be ashamed about going before the throne of God to seek out His wisdom concerning your spouse. Your marriage will be for the better and your Father in Heaven would never deny this petition and be timely to fulfill it. We as soon to be wives should practice going before our Father in heaven daily, seeking wisdom for our future marriages so that when they come, we are prepared with a solid foundation beforehand and do not struggle as much when challenges and situations arrive. Remember that "two shall become one", you will learn to put the other person before yourself, a solid wise foundation will make the transition from individual thinking to one part of a whole thinking smoother. Rely on the wisdom of God and the leading of Holy Spirit.